SACRAMENTS AND ORTHODOXY

SACRAMENTS AND ORTHODOXY

ALEXANDER SCHMEMANN

HERDER AND HERDER

1965
HERDER AND HERDER NEW YORK
232 Madison Avenue, New York 10016

Library of Congress Catalog Card Number: 65–13482

Contents

INTRODUCTION

The purpose of this book, written by an Eastern Orthodox priest, is to contribute, be it only partially and in a modest way, to the great spiritual debate in which today all Christians are involved on the place of Christianity in our modern world. The book is an attempt to relate the world's problems, hopes and difficulties to the sacramental experience which has always constituted the very heart of the Orthodox worldview, to indicate the cosmic and catholic, i.e. the all-embracing, all-assuming and all-transforming nature and scope of Christian *leitourgia*.

But if the source of all that I am trying to convey in these pages is in the liturgical tradition of Eastern Orthodoxy, I am also fully aware of my deep indebtedness to the spiritual and theological revival that has so decisively marked the Christian West in our time and, more particularly, to the liturgical movement. It is this indebtedness that I want to acknowledge in this brief introduction.

For several centuries the two initial "halves" of Christianity, as it appeared in history, the Eastern and the Western, lived not only in ecclesiastical and doctrinal separation from one another, but also in almost complete mutal ignorance of one another. And although we certainly view

and explain differently the causes and the nature of our
divisions, no one would deny today that one of their most
tragic results was that they developed, within each of their
separated "worlds," a sense of self-sufficiency which led, in
turn, to a narrowing of spiritual vision and an impoverish-
ment of theological perspective. There was much polemic,
but no effort to understand; many accusations, but no real
interest; two monologues rather than a dialogue. And it is
not an exaggerated to affirm that it was precisely the liturgical movement which, even before the organized ecumenical movement began, was the first to break through the
ignorance and indifference, to create the possibility of a
new encounter, no longer in fear and suspicion, but in love
and mutual respect and, above all, on a common ground.
The work of men such as Odo Casel and Lambert Beauduin,
J. A. Jungmann and Louis Bouyer, Romano Guardini and
H. A. Reinhold—to name but a few among so many, did
more than merely initiate a liturgical revival within Roman
Catholicism. It helped to establish a common theological
and spiritual perspective, to restore a truly catholic language without which no fruitful encounter, no ecumenical
conversation is possible. Their writings were and still are as
significant for us Orthodox as they are for our Western
brothers. For not only did they help us better to understand
the liturgical and spiritual heritage of the West, they also
helped us—paradoxically as it sounds—to understand better
our own *lex orandi*. This does not mean agreement on all
points, but with men such as these even disagreements have
become meaningful and constructive. For, by raising the

right questions, by placing the study of the liturgy in a missionary, theological and ecumenical perspective, and, above all, by their spirit of charity they traced the way which we must acknowledge as our common way. To all of them, whether they are alive or asleep in the Lord, I am happy to dedicate this little book.

All this makes clear, I hope, that the following pages are not meant to be an Orthodox "lesson" to the West. Positions and attitudes criticized here are not the monopoly of any one ecclesiastical or geographical area, just as the ideas proposed and defended here, if I find them in my Orthodox faith and worship, have had everywhere much better and more qualified exponents. I am not trying, of course, to obliterate or minimize the areas of doctrinal disagreements, for to do so would be in contradiction with the very foundations of a truly ecumenical spirit. Ecumenism means not a relativistic attitude, not a compromise, but, first of all, the readiness to listen and to be listened to, to make the search for truth—difficult and painful as it may be—a common task.

This book was originally written and made available in a limited edition as a study guide for a conference of the World Christian Student Federation. It is not aimed at theologians and therefore has no academic apparatus. It is my hope, however, that in this popular form it may be of spiritual benefit to its readers.

1 THE LIFE OF THE WORLD

Man is what he eats." With this statement the German materialistic philosopher Feuerbach thought he had put an end to all "idealistic" speculations about human nature. In fact, however, he was expressing, without knowing it, the most religious idea of man. For long before Feuerbach the same definition of man was given by the Bible. In the biblical story of creation man is presented, first of all, as a hungry being, and the whole world as his food. Second only to the direction to propagate and have dominion over the earth, according to the author of the first chapter of Genesis, God instructs men to eat of the earth: "Behold I have given you every herb bearing seed . . . and every tree, which is the fruit of a tree yielding seed; to you it shall be for meat. . . ." Man must eat in order to live; he must take the world into his body and transform it into himself, into flesh and blood. He is indeed that which he eats, and the whole world is presented as one all-embracing banquet table for man. And this image of the banquet remains, throughout the whole Bible, the central image of life. It is the image of life at its creation and also the image of life at its end and fulfillment: ". . . that you eat and drink at my table in my Kingdom."

I begin with this seemingly secondary theme of food—
secondary from the standpoint of the great "religious issues" of our time—because the very purpose of this essay
is to answer, if possible, the question: of what life do we
speak, what life do we preach, proclaim and announce
when, as Christians, we confess that Christ died for the life
of the world? What *life* is both motivation, and the beginning and the goal of Christian *mission*?

The existing answers follow two general patterns. There
are those among us for whom life, when discussed in religious terms, means *religious life*. And this religious life is a
world in itself, existing apart from the secular world and its
life. It is the world of "spirituality," and in our days it
seems to gain more and more popularity. Even the airport
bookstands are filled with anthologies of mystical writings.
Basic Mysticism is a title we saw on one of them. Lost and
confused in the noise, the rush and the frustrations of
"life," man easily accepts the invitation to enter into the
inner sanctuary of his soul and to discover there another
life, to enjoy a "spiritual banquet" amply supplied with
spiritual food. This spiritual food will *help* him. It will help
him to restore his peace of mind, to endure the other—the
"secular"—life, to accept its tribulations, to lead a whole-
some and more dedicated life, to "keep smiling" in a deep,
religious way. And thus *mission* consists here in converting
people to this "spiritual" life, in making them religious.

There exists a great variety of emphases and even theologies within this general pattern, from the popular revival
to the sophisticated interest in esoteric mystical doctrines.

But the result is the same: "religious" life makes the secular one—the life of eating and drinking—irrelevant, deprives it of any real meaning save that of being an exercise in piety and patience. And the more spiritual is the "religious banquet," the more secular and material become the neon lighted signs EAT, DRINK that we see along our highways.

But there are those also, to whom the affirmation "for the life of the world" seems to mean naturally "for the better life of the world." The "spiritualists" are counterbalanced by the activists. To be sure we are far today from the simple optimism and euphoria of the "Social Gospel." All the implications of existentialism with its anxieties, of neo-Orthodoxy with its pessimistic and realistic view of history have been assimilated and given proper consideration. But the fundamental belief in Christianity as being first of all action has remained intact, and in fact has acquired a new strength. From this point of view Christianity has simply lost the world. And the world must be recovered. The Christian mission, therefore, is to catch up with the life that has gone astray. The "eating" and "drinking" man is taken quite seriously, almost too seriously. He constitutes the virtually exclusive object of Christian action, and we are constantly called to repent for having spent too much time in contemplation and adoration, in silence and liturgy, for having not dealt sufficiently with the social, political, economic, racial and all other issues of real life. To books on mysticism and spirituality correspond books on "Religion and Life" (or Society, or Urbanism or Sex . . .). And yet the basic question remains unanswered: what is this *life* that we must regain for Christ, make Christian? What is, in other words, the ultimate end of all this doing and action?

Suppose we have reached at least one of these practical goals, have "won"—then what? The question may seem a naive one, but one cannot really act and do, without knowing the meaning not only of action, but of the life itself in the name of which one acts. One eats and drinks, one fights for freedom and justice in order to be *alive*, to have the *fullness of life*. But what is it? What is the life of life itself? What is the content of life eternal? At some ultimate point, within some ultimate analysis, we inescapably discover that in and by itself action has no meaning. When all committees have fulfilled their task, all papers have been distributed and all practical goals achieved, there must come a perfect joy. About what? Unless we know, the same dichotomy between religion and life, which we have mentioned in the spiritual solution, remains. Whether we "spiritualize" our life or "secularize" our religion, whether we invite men to a spiritual banquet or simply join them at the secular one, the real life of the world, for which we are told God gave his only begotten Son, remains hopelessly beyond our religious grasp.

2

Man is what he eats." But what does he eat and why? These questions seem naive and irrelevant not only to Feuerbach. They seemed even more irrelevant to his religious opponents. To them, as to him, eating was a material function, and the only important question was whether in addition to it man possessed a spiritual "superstructure." Religion said yes. Feuerbach said no. But both answers were given within the same fundamental opposition of the spiritual to the material. "Spiritual" *versus* "material," "sacred" *versus* "profane," "supernatural" *versus* "natural"—such were for centuries the only accepted, the only understandable moulds and categories of religious thought and experience. And Feuerbach, for all his materialism, was in fact a natural heir to Christian "idealism" and "spiritualism."

But the Bible, we have seen, also begins with man as a hungry being, with the man who is that which he eats. The perspective, however, is wholly different, for nowhere in the Bible do we find the dichotomies which for us are the self-evident framework of all approaches to religion. In the Bible the food that man eats, the world of which he must partake in order to live, is given to him by God, and it is given as *communion with God*. The world as man's food is not something "material" and limited to material functions, thus being different from, and opposed to, the specifically "spiritual" functions by which man is related to God. All that exists is God's gift to man, and it all exists to make God known to man, to make man's life communion with God. It is divine love made food, made life for man. God *blesses* everything he creates, and, in biblical language, this means that he makes all creation the sign and means of his presence and wisdom, love and revelation. "O taste and see how gracious the Lord is."

Man is a hungry being. But he is hungry for God. Behind all the hunger of our life is God. All desire is finally a desire for him. To be sure, man is not the only hungry being. All that exists lives by "eating." The whole creation depends on food. But the unique position of man in the universe is that he alone is to bless God for the food and the life he receives from Him. He alone is to respond to God's blessing with his blessing. The significant fact about the life in the Garden is that man is to name things. As soon as animals have been created to keep Adam company, God brings them to Adam to see what he will call them. "And whatsoever Adam called every living creature, that was the name thereof." Now, in the Bible a name is infinitely more than a means to distinguish one thing from another. It reveals the very essence of a thing, or rather its essence as God's gift. To name a thing is to manifest the meaning and value God gave it, to know it as coming from God and to know its place and function within the cosmos created by God.

To name a thing, in other words, is to bless God for it and in it. And in the Bible to bless God is not a "religious" or a "cultic" act, but the very way of life. God blessed the world, blessed the man, blessed the seventh day (that is, time), and this means that he filled all that exists with His love and goodness, made all this "very good." So the only natural (and not "supernatural") reaction of man, to whom God gave this blessed and sanctified world, is to bless God in return, to thank him, to see the world as God sees it— and in this act of gratitude and adoration—to know, name and possess the world. All rational, spiritual and other qualities of man, distinguishing him from other creatures, have their focus and ultimate fulfillment in this capacity to bless God, to know, so to speak, the meaning of the thirst and hunger that constitutes his life. "Homo sapiens," "homo faber" . . . yes, but, first of all, "homo adorans." The first, the basic definition of man is that he is the priest. He stands in the center of the world and unifies it in his act of blessing God, of both receiving the world from God and offering it to God—and by filling the world with this eucharist, he transforms his life, the one that he receives from the world, into life in God, into communion.

The world was created as the "matter," the material of one all-embracing eucharist, and man was created as the priest of this cosmic sacrament.

Men understand all this instinctively if not rationally. Centuries of secularism have failed to transform eating into something strictly utilitarian. Food is still treated with reverence. A meal is still a rite—the last "natural sacrament" of family and friendship, of life that is more than "eating" and "drinking." To eat is still something more than to maintain bodily functions. People may not understand what that "something more" is, but they nonetheless desire to celebrate it. They are still hungry and thirsty for sacramental life.

3

It is not accidental, therefore, that the biblical story of the Fall is centered again on food. Man ate the forbidden fruit. The fruit of that one tree, whatever else it may signify, was

unlike every other fruit in the Garden: it was not offered as
a gift to man. Not given, not blessed by God, it was food
whose eating was condemned to be communion with itself
alone, and not with God. It is the image of the world loved
for itself, and eating it is the image of life understood as
an end in itself.

To love is not easy, and mankind has chosen not to return God's love. Man has loved the world, but as an end in
itself and not as transparent to God. He has done it so con-
sistently that it has become something that is "in the air."
It seems natural for man to experience the world as opaque,
and not shot through with the presence of God. It seems
natural not to live a life of thanksgiving for God's gift of a
world. It seems natural not to be eucharistic.

The world is a fallen world because it has fallen away
from the awareness that God is all in all. The accumulation
of this disregard for God is the original sin that blights the
world. And even the religion of this fallen world cannot
heal or redeem it, for it has accepted the reduction of God
to an area called "sacred" ("spiritual," "supernatural")—as
opposed to the world as "profane." It has accepted the all-
embracing secularism which attempts to steal the world
away from God.

The natural dependence of man upon the world was intended to be transformed constantly into communion with
God in whom is all life. Man was to be the priest of a
eucharist, offering the world to God, and in this offering he
was to receive the gift of life. But in the fallen world man
does not have the priestly power to do this. His dependence
on the world becomes a closed circuit, and his love is de-

viated from its true direction. He still loves, he is still hungry. He knows he is dependent on that which is beyond him. But his love and his dependence refer only to the world in itself. He does not know that breathing can be communion with God. He does not realize that to eat can be to receive life from God in more than its physical sense. He forgets that the world, its air or its food cannot by themselves bring life, but only as they are received and accepted for God's sake, in God and as bearers of the divine gift of life. By themselves they can produce only the appearance of life.

When we see the world as an end in itself, everything becomes itself a value and consequently loses all value, because only in God is found the meaning (value) of everything, and the world is meaningful only when it is the "sacrament" of God's presence. Things treated merely as things in themselves destroy themselves because only in God have they any life. The world of nature, cut off from the source of life, is a dying world. For one who thinks food in itself is the source of life, eating is communion with the dying world, it is communion with death. Food itself is dead, it is life that has died and it must be kept in refrigerators like a corpse.

For "the ransom of sin is death." The life man chose was only the appearance of life. God showed him that he himself had decided to eat bread in a way that would simply return him to the ground from which both he and the bread had been taken: "For dust thou art and into dust shalt thou return." Man lost the eucharistic life, he lost the life of life itself, the power to transform it into Life. He ceased to be the priest of the world and became its slave.

In the story of the Garden this took place in the cool of the day: that is, at night. And Adam, when he left the Garden where life was to have been eucharistic—an offering of the world in thanksgiving to God—Adam led the whole world, as it were, into darkness. In one of the beautiful pieces of Byzantine hymnology Adam is pictured sitting outside, facing Paradise, weeping. It is the figure of man himself.

4

We can interrupt here for a while this theme of food. We began with it only in order to free the terms "sacramental" and "eucharistic" from the connotations they have acquired in the long history of technical theology, where they are applied almost exclusively within the framework of "natural" versus "supernatural," and "sacred" versus "profane," that is, within the same opposition between religion and life which makes life ultimately unredeemable and religiously meaningless. In our perspective, however, the "original" sin is not primarily that man has "disobeyed" God; the sin is that he ceased to be hungry for him and for him alone, ceased to see his whole life depending on the whole world as a sacrament of communion with God. The sin was not that man neglected his religious duties. The sin was that he thought of God in terms of religion, i.e. opposing him to life. The only real fall of man is his non-

eucharistic life in a noneucharistic world. The fall is not
that he preferred world to God, distorted the balance between the spiritual and material, but that he made the
world *material*, whereas he was to have transformed it into
"life in God," filled it with meaning and spirit.

But it is the Christian gospel that God did not leave
man in his exile, in the predicament of confused longing.
He had created man "after his own heart" and for himself,
and man has struggled in his freedom to find the answer to
the mysterious hunger in him. In this scene of radical un-
fulfillment God acted decisively: into the darkness where
man was groping toward Paradise, he sent light. He did so
not as a rescue operation, to recover lost man: it was rather
for the completing of what he had undertaken from the
beginning. God acted so that man might understand who
he really was and where his hunger had been driving him.

The light God sent was his Son: the same light that had
been shining unextinguished in the world's darkness all
along, seen now in full brightness.

Before Christ came, God had promised him to man. He
had done so in major fashion, speaking through the prophets of Israel, but also in those many other ways in which he
corresponds with man. As Christians we believe that he,
who is the truth about both God and man, gives foretaste
of his incarnation in all more fragmentary truths. We believe as well that Christ is present in any seeker after truth.
Simone Weil has said that though a person runs as fast as
he can away from Christ, if it is toward what he considers
true, he runs in fact straight into the arms of Christ.

Much that is true of God has also been revealed in the long history of religion, and this can be demonstrated for the Christian by reference to the true standard of Christ. In the great religions which have given shape to human aspirations, God plays on an orchestra which is far out of tune, yet there has often been a marvelous, rich music made.

Christianity, however, is in a profound sense the end of all religion. In the Gospel story of the Samaritan woman at the well, Jesus made this clear. " 'Sir,' the woman said to him, 'I perceive that thou art a prophet. Our fathers worshipped in this mountain; and ye say, that in Jerusalem is the place when men ought to worship.' Jesus saith unto her, 'Woman, believe me, the hour cometh, when ye shall neither in this mountain, nor yet at Jerusalem, worship the Father. . . . But the hour cometh, and now is, when the true worshippers shall worship the Father in spirit and in truth: for the Father seeketh such to worship him' " (Jn 4:19–21, 23). She asked him a question about cult, and in reply Jesus changed the whole perspective of the matter. Nowhere in the New Testament, in fact, is Christianity presented as a cult or as a religion. Religion is needed where there is a wall of separation between God and man. But Christ who is both God and man, has broken down the wall between man and God. He has inaugurated a new life, not a new religion.

It was this freedom of the early church from "religion" in the usual, traditional sense of this word, that led the pagans into accusing Christians of atheism. Christians had no concern for any sacred geography, no temples, no cult that could be recognized as such by the generations fed in the solemnities of the mystery cults. There was no specific religious interest in the places where Jesus had lived. There were no pilgrimages. The old religion had its thousand sacred places and temples: for the Christians all this was past and gone. There was no need for temples built of stone: Christ's Body, the Church itself, the new people gathered in him, was the only real temple. "Destroy this temple, and in three days I will raise it up. . . ." (Jn 2:19).

The Church itself was the new and heavenly Jerusalem: the Church in Jerusalem was by contrast unimportant. The fact that Christ comes and is present was far more significant than the places where he had been. The historical reality of Christ was of course the undisputed ground of the early Christians' faith: yet they did not so much remember him as know he was with them. And in him was the end of "religion," because he himself was the Answer to all religion, to all human hunger for God, because in him the life that was lost by man—and which could only be symbolized, signified, asked for in religion—was restored to man.

5

This is not a treatise of systematic theology. It does not attempt to explore all the aspects and implications of this Answer. Nor does it pretend to add anything—in this small scope—to the wisdom accumulated in innumerable volumes of "theologies" and "dogmatics." The purpose of this book is a humble one. It is to remind its readers that in Christ, life—life in all its totality—was returned to man, given again as sacrament and communion, made Eucharist. And it is to show—be it only partially and superficially—the meaning of this for our mission in the world. The Western Christian is used to thinking of sacrament as opposed to the word and links the mission with the Word and not the sacrament. He is, moreover, accustomed to consider the sacrament as, maybe, an essential and yet clearly defined part or institution or act of the Church and within the Church, but not of the Church as being itself the sacrament of Christ's presence and action. And finally he is primarily interested in certain very "formal" questions concerning the sacraments: their number, their "validity," their institution, etc. Our purpose is to show that there exists and always existed a different perspective, a different approach to the sacrament and that this approach may be of crucial importance precisely for the whole burning issue of mission, of our witness to Christ in the world. For the basic question is: *of what are we witnesses?* What have we seen, touched with our hands? Of what have we partaken, been made communicants? Where do we call men? What can we offer them?

This essay is written by an Eastern Orthodox and in the perspective of the Orthodox Church. But it is not a book about Eastern Orthodoxy, as the books about Orthodoxy are written and understood today. There exists a "Western" approach to the East which the Orthodox themselves have accepted. Orthodoxy is presented usually as the specialist in "mysticism" and "spirituality," as the potential home of all those who thirst and hunger for the "spiritual banquet." The Orthodox Church has been assigned the place and the function of the "liturgical" and "sacramental" church, *therefore* more or less indifferent to the mission. But all this is wrong. The Orthodox may have failed much too often to see the real implications of their "sacramentalism," but its fundamental meaning is certainly not that of escaping into a timeless "spirituality" far from the dull world of "action." And it is this true meaning that this book would like to disclose and share with its readers.

Beautiful churches with "all night vigil services," icons and processions, a liturgy, which to be properly performed requires not less than twenty-seven heavy liturgical books— all this seems to contradict what has been said above about Christianity as the "end of religion." But does it in fact? And if not, what is the *meaning* of all this in the real world in which we live, and for the life of which God has given his Son?

2   THE EUCHARIST

In this world Christ was rejected. He was the perfect expression of life as God intended it. The fragmentary life of the world was gathered into his life; He was the heart beat of the world and the world killed him. But in that murder the world itself died. It lost its last chance to become the paradise God created it to be. We can go on developing new and better material things. We can build a more humane society which may even keep us from annihilating each other. But when Christ, the true life of the world was rejected, it was the beginning of the end. That rejection had a finality about it: He was crucified for good. As Pascal said: "Christ is in agony until the end of the world."

Christianity often appears, however, to preach that if men will try hard enough to live Christian lives, the crucifixion can somehow be reversed. This is because Christianity has forgotten itself, forgotten that always it must first of all stand at the cross. Not that this world cannot be improved. One of our goals is certainly to work for peace, justice, freedom. But while it can be improved, it can never become the place God intended it to be. Christianity does not condemn the world. The world has condemned itself when on Calvary it condemned the One who was its true self. "He was in the world, and the world was made by him, and the world knew him not" (Jn 1:10). If we think seriously—about the real meaning, the real scope of these words—we know that as Christians and insofar as we are Christians we are, first of all, witnesses of that end; end of all natural joy; end of all satisfaction of man with the world and with himself; end, indeed, of life itself as a reasonable and reasonably organized "pursuit of happiness." Christians did not have to wait for the modern proponents of existentialist anxiety, despair and absurdity to be aware of all this. And although in the course of their long history Christians have much too often forgotten the meaning of the cross, and enjoyed life as if "nothing had happened," although each one of us too often takes "time off"—we know that in the world in which Christ died, "natural life" has been brought to its end.

2

And yet, from its very beginning Christianity has been the proclamation of joy, of the only possible joy on earth. It rendered impossible all joy we usually think of as possible. But within this impossibility, at the very bottom of this darkness, it announced and conveyed a new all-embracing joy, and with this joy it transformed the End into a Beginning. Without the proclamation of this joy Christianity is incomprehensible. It is only as joy that the Church was victorious in the world and it lost the world when it lost the joy, when it ceased to be a witness of it. Of all accusations against Christians, the most terrible one was uttered by Nietzsche when he said that Christians had no joy. . . .

Let us, therefore, forget for a while the technical discussions about the Church, its mission, its methods. Not that these discussions are wrong or unnecessary. But they can be useful and meaningful only within a fundamental context, and that context is the "great joy" from which everything else in Christianity developed and acquired its meaning. "For, behold, I bring you good tidings of great joy"—thus begins the Gospel, and its end is: "And they worshipped him and returned to Jerusalem with great joy. . . ." (Lk 2:10, 24:52). And we must recover the meaning of this great joy. We must if possible partake of it, before we discuss anything else—programs and missions, projects and techniques.

Joy, however, is not something one can define or analyze. One enters into joy. "Enter thou into the joy of thy Lord" (Mt 25:21). And we have no other means of entering into that joy, no way of understanding it, except through the one action which from the beginning has been for the Church both the source and the fulfillment of joy, the very sacrament of joy, the Eucharist.

The Eucharist is a liturgy. And he who says *liturgy* today is likely to get involved in a controversy. For to some—the "liturgically minded"—of all the activities of the Church, liturgy is the most important, if not the only one. To others, liturgy is esthetic and spiritual deviation from the real task of the Church. There exist today "liturgical" and "non-liturgical" churches and Christians. But this controversy is unnecessary for it has its roots in one basic misunderstanding—the "liturgical" understanding of the liturgy. This is the reduction of the liturgy to "cultic" categories, its definition as a sacred act of worship, different as such not only from the "profane" area of life, but even from all other activities of the Church itself. But this is not the original meaning of the Greek word *leitourgia*. It meant an action by which a group of people become something corporately which they had not been as a mere collection of individuals —a whole greater than the sum of its parts. It meant also a function or "ministry" of a man or of a group on behalf of and in the interest of the whole community. Thus the *leitourgia* of ancient Israel was the corporate work of a chosen few to prepare the world for the coming of the Messiah. And in this very act of preparation they became what they were called to be, the Israel of God, the chosen instrument of his purpose.

Thus the Church itself is a *leitourgia*, a ministry, a calling to act in this world after the fashion of Christ, to bear testimony to him and his kingdom. The eucharistic liturgy, therefore, must not be approached and understood in "liturgical" or "cultic" terms alone. Just as Christianity can —and must—be considered the end of religion, so the Christian liturgy in general, and the Eucharist in particular, are indeed the end of cult, of the "sacred" religious act isolated from, and opposed to, the "profane" life of the community. The first condition for the understanding of liturgy is to forget about any specific "liturgical piety."

The Eucharist is a sacrament. But he who says sacrament

also gets involved in a controversy. If we speak of sacrament, where is the Word? Are we not leading ourselves into the dangers of "sacramentalism" and "magic," into a betrayal of the spiritual character of Christianity? To these questions, no answer can be given at this point. For the whole purpose of this essay is to show that the context within which such questions are being asked is not the only possible one. At this stage we shall say only this: the Eucharist is the entrance of the Church into the joy of its Lord. And to enter into that joy, so as to be a witness to it in the world, is indeed the very calling of the Church, its essential *leitourgia*, the sacrament by which it "becomes what it is."

In the brief description of the Eucharist which follows, references will be made primarily to the Orthodox eucharistic liturgy, and this for two reasons. First, in the area of liturgy one can speak with conviction only insofar as one has experienced that about which one is speaking. This author's experience has been in the Orthodox tradition. And second, it is the unanimous opinion of "liturgiologists" that the Orthodox liturgy has best preserved those elements and emphases which constitute the very theme of this book.

3

The liturgy of the Eucharist is best understood as a journey or procession. It is the journey of the Church into the dimension of the kingdom. We use this word "dimension" because it seems the best way to indicate the manner of our sacramental entrance into the risen life of Christ. Color transparencies "come alive" when viewed in three dimensions instead of two. The presence of the added dimension allows us to see much more the actual reality of what has been photographed. In very much the same way, though of course any analogy is condemned to fail, our entrance into the presence of Christ is an entrance into a fourth dimension which allows us to see the ultimate reality of life. It is not an escape from the world, rather it is the arrival at a vantage point from which we can see more deeply into the reality of the world.

The journey begins when Christians leave their homes and beds. They leave, indeed, their life in this present and concrete world, and whether they have to drive fifteen miles or walk a few blocks, a sacramental act is already taking place, an act which is the very condition of everything else that is to happen. For they are now on their way to constitute the Church, or to be more exact, to be transformed into the Church of God. They have been individuals, some white, some black, some poor, some rich, they have been the "natural" world and a natural community. And now they have been called to "come together in one place," to bring their lives, their very "world" with them and to be more than what they were: a new community with a new life. We are already far beyond the categories of common worship and prayer. The purpose of this "coming together" is not simply to add a religious dimension to the natural community, to make it "better"—more responsible, more Christian. The purpose is to fulfill the Church and that means to "re-present," to make present the One, in whom all things are at their end, and all things are at their *beginning*.

The liturgy begins then as a real separation from the world. In our attempt to make Christianity appeal to the man on the street, we have often minimized, or even completely forgotten, this necessary separation. We always want to make Christianity "understandable" and "acceptable" to this mythical "modern" man on the street. And we forget that the Christ of whom we speak is "not of this world" and that after his resurrection he was not recognized even by his own disciples. Mary Magdalene thought he was a gardener. When two of his disciples were going to Emmaus, "Jesus himself drew near and went with them" . . . and they did not know him before "he took bread, and blessed it, and brake, and gave it to them" (Lk 24:15–16, 30). He appeared to the twelve, "the doors being shut." It was apparently no longer sufficient simply to know that he was the son of Mary. There was no physical imperative to recognize him. He was, in other words, no longer a "part" of this world, of its reality, and to recognize him, to enter into the joy of his presence, to be with him meant a conversion to another reality. The Lord's glorification does not have the compelling, objective evidence of his humiliation and cross. His glorification is known only through the mysterious death in the baptismal font, through the anointing of the Holy Spirit. It is known only in the fullness of the Church, as she gathers to meet the Lord and to share in his risen life.

The early Christians realized that in order to become the temple of the Holy Spirit, they must *ascend to heaven* where Christ has ascended. They realized also that this ascension was the very condition of their mission in the world, of their ministry to the world. For there—in heaven —they were immersed in the new life of the Kingdom; and when after this "liturgy of ascension," they returned into the world, their faces reflected the light, the "joy and peace" of that Kingdom and they were truly its witnesses. They brought no programs and no theories; but wherever they went, the seeds of the Kingdom sprouted, faith was kindled, life was transfigured, things impossible were made possible. They were witnesses, and when they were asked: "Whence shines this light, where is the source of this power?" they knew what to answer and where to lead men. In church today, we so often find we meet only the same old world, not Christ and his kingdom. We do not realize that we never get anywhere because we never leave any place behind us.

To leave, to come. . . . This is the *beginning*, the starting point of the sacrament, the condition of its transforming power and reality.

4

The Orthodox liturgy begins with the solemn doxology: "Blessed is the Kingdom of the Father, the Son and the Holy Spirit, now and ever, and unto ages on ages." From the beginning the destination is announced: the journey is

to the Kingdom. This is where we are going—and not sym-
bolically, but really. In the language of the Bible, which is
the language of the Church, to bless the Kingdom is not
simply to acclaim it. It is to declare it to be the goal, the
end of all our desires and interests, of our whole life, the
supreme and ultimate value of all that exists. To bless is to
accept in love, and to move toward what is loved and accepted. The Church thus is the assembly, the gathering of
those to whom the ultimate destination of all life has been
revealed and who have accepted it. This acceptance is expressed in the solemn answer to the doxology: Amen. It is
indeed one of the most important words in the world, for
it expresses the agreement of the Church to follow Christ
in his ascension to his Father, to make this ascension the
destiny of man. It is Christ's gift to us, for only in him can
we say Amen to God, or rather he himself is our Amen to
God and the Church is an Amen to Christ. Upon this
Amen the fate of the human race is decided. It reveals that
the movement toward God has begun.

But we are still at the very beginning. We have left "this
world." We have come together. We have heard the announcement of our ultimate destination. We have said
Amen to this announcement. We are the ecclesia, the response to this call and order. And we begin with "common
prayers and supplications," with a common and joyful act
of praise. Once more, the joyful character of the eucharistic
gathering must be stressed. For the medieval emphasis on
the cross while not a wrong one, is certainly one-sided. The
liturgy is, before everything else, the joyous gathering of

those who are to meet the risen Lord and to enter with him into the bridal chamber. And it is this joy of expectation and this expectation of joy that are expressed in singing and ritual, in vestments and in censing, in that whole "beauty" of the liturgy, which has so often been denounced as unnecessary and even sinful.

Unnecessary it is, indeed, for we are beyond the categories of the "necessary." Beauty is never "necessary," "functional" or "useful." And when, expecting someone whom we love, we put a beautiful tablecloth on the table and decorate it with candles and flowers, we do all this not out of necessity, but out of love. And the Church is love, expectation and joy. It is heaven on earth, according to our Orthodox tradition; it is the joy of recovered childhood, that free, unconditioned and disinterested joy which alone is capable of transforming the world. In our adult, serious piety we ask for definitions and justifications, and they are rooted in fear. Fear of corruption, deviation, "pagan influences," what not. But "he that feareth is not made perfect in love" (1 Jn 4:18). As long as Christians will love the Kingdom of God, and not only discuss it, they will "represent" it and signify it, in art and beauty. And the celebrant of the sacrament of joy will appear in a beautiful chasuble, because he is vested in the glory of the Kingdom, because even in the form of man God appears in glory. In the Eucharist we are standing in the presence of Christ, and like Moses before God, we are to be covered with his glory. Christ himself wore an unsewn garment which the soldiers at the cross did not divide: it had not been bought in the

market, but in all likelihood it had been fashioned by someone's loving hands. Yes, the beauty of our preparation for
the Eucharist has no practical use. But Romano Guardini
has spoken wisely of this useless beauty. In the liturgy he
says:

Man, with the aid of grace, is given the opportunity of re-
laying his fundamental essence, of really becoming that which
according to his divine destiny he should be and longs to be, a
child of God. In the liturgy he is to go "unto God, who giveth
joy to his youth." . . . Because the life of the liturgy is higher
than that to which customary reality gives either the opportunity
or form of expression, it adapts suitable forms and methods
from that sphere in which alone they are to be found, that is
to say, from art. It speaks measuredly and melodiously; it em-
ploys formal, rhythmic gestures; it is clothed in colors and
garments foreign to everyday life. . . . It is in the highest sense
the life of a child, in which everything is picture, melody and
song. Such is the wonderful fact which the liturgy demon-
strates: it unites act and reality in a supernatural childhood
before God.[1]

5

The next act of the liturgy is the *entrance*: the coming of
the celebrant to the altar. It has been given all possible
symbolical explanations, but it is not a "symbol." It is the
very movement of the Church as *passage* from the old into
the new, from "this world" into the "world to come" and,
as such, it is the essential movement of the liturgical "journey." In "this world" there is no altar and the temple has

[1] Romano Guardini, *The Church ·and the Catholic, and the
Spirit of the Liturgy*, New York 1950, 180–181.

been destroyed. For the only altar is Christ himself, his humanity—which he has assumed and deified and made the temple of God, the altar of his presence. And Christ has ascended into heaven. The altar, thus, is the sign that in Christ we have been given access to heaven, that the Church is the "passage" to heaven, the entrance into the heavenly sanctuary, and that only by "entering," by ascending to heaven does the Church fulfill itself, become what it is. And so, the entrance at the Eucharist, this approach of the celebrant—and in him, of the whole Church—to the altar is not a symbol. It is the crucial and decisive act in which the true dimensions of the sacrament are revealed and established. It is not "grace" that comes down; it is the Church that enters into "grace," and grace means the new being, the Kingdom, the world to come. And as the celebrant approaches the altar, the Church intones the hymn which the angels eternally sing at the throne of God: Holy God, Holy Mighty, Holy Immortal . . . and the priest says: "Holy God, who art praised with the thrice holy voice of the Seraphim, glorified by the Cherubim and adored by all the hosts of heaven. . . ."

The angels are not here for decoration and inspiration. They stand precisely for heaven, for that glorious and incomprehensible beyond and above, of which we know only one thing: that it eternally resounds with the praise of divine glory and holiness. "Holy . . ." is the real name of God, of the God "not of scholars and philosophers," but the living God of faith. The knowledge about God results in definitions and distinctions. The knowledge of God leads to this one, incomprehensible, yet obvious and inescapable word: holy. And in this word we express both that God is the Absolutely Other, the one *about* whom we know nothing, and that he is the end of all our hunger, all our desires, the inaccessible one who mobilizes our wills, the mysterious treasure that attracts us, and there is really nothing to know but him. "Holy" is the word, the song, the "reaction" of the Church as it enters into heaven, as it stands before the heavenly glory of God.

6

Now, for the first time since the eucharistic journey began, the celebrant turns back and faces the people. Up to this moment he was the one who led the Church in its ascension, but now the movement has reached its goal. And the priest whose liturgy, whose unique function and obedience in the Church is to re-present, to make present the priesthood of Christ himself, says to the people: "Peace be with you." In Christ man returns to God and in Christ God comes to man. As the new Adam, as the perfect man he leads us to God; as God incarnate he reveals the Father to us and reconciles us with God. He is our *peace*—the reconciliation with God, divine forgiveness, communion. And the peace that the priest announces and bestows upon us is the peace Christ has established between God and his world and into which we, the Church, have entered.

It is within this peace—"which passeth all understanding"—that now begins the liturgy of the Word. Western

Christians are so accustomed to distinguish the Word from the sacrament that it may be difficult for them to understand that in the Orthodox perspective the liturgy of the Word is as sacramental as the sacrament is "evangelical." The sacrament is a manifestation of the Word. And unless the false dichotomy between Word and sacrament is overcome, the true meaning of both Word and sacrament, and especially the true meaning of Christian "sacramentalism" cannot be grasped in all their wonderful implications. The proclamation of the Word is a sacramental act par excellence because it is a transforming act. It transforms the human words of the Gospel into the Word of God and the manifestation of the Kingdom. And it transforms the man who hears the Word into a receptacle of the Word and a temple of the Spirit. . . . Each Saturday night, at the solemn resurrection vigil, the book of the Gospel is brought in a solemn procession to the midst of the congregation and in this act the Lord's Day is announced and manifested. For the Gospel is not only a "record" of Christ's resurrection; the Word of God is the eternal coming to us of the Risen Lord, the very power and joy of the resurrection.

In the liturgy the proclamation of the Gospel is preceded by "Alleluia," the singing of this mysterious "theoforous" (God-bearing) word which is the joyful greeting of those who see the coming Lord, who know his presence, and who express their joy at this glorious "parousia." "Here he is!" might be a poor, yet an almost adequate translation of this untranslatable word.

This is why the reading and the preaching of the Gospel

in the Orthodox Church is a *liturgical act*, an integral and essential part of the sacrament. It is heard as Word of God, and it is received in the Spirit—that is, in the Church, which is the life of the Word and its "growth" in the world.

7

Bread and wine: to understand their initial and eternal meaning in the Eucharist, we must forget for a time the endless controversies which little by little transformed them into "elements" of an almost abstract theological speculation. It is indeed one of the main defects of sacramental theology that instead of following the order of the eucharistic journey with its progressive revelation of meaning, theologians applied to the Eucharist a set of abstract questions in order to squeeze it into their own intellectual framework. In this approach what virtually disappeared from the sphere of theological interest and investigation was liturgy itself and what remained were isolated "moments," "formulas" and "conditions of validity." What disappeared was the Eucharist as one organic, all-embracing and all-transforming act of the whole Church and what remained were: "essential" and "nonessential" parts, "elements," "consecration," etc. Thus, for example, to explain and define the meaning of the Eucharist the way certain theology does it, there is no need for the word "eucharist"; it becomes irrelevant. And yet for the early Fathers it was the key word giving unity and meaning to all the "elements" of the liturgy. The Fathers called "eucharist" the bread and wine of the offering, and their offering and consecration, and finally, communion. All this was *Eucharist* and all this could be understood only within the Eucharist.

As we proceed further in the eucharistic liturgy, the time has come now to offer to God the totality of all our lives, of ourselves, of the world in which we live. This is the first meaning of our bringing to the altar the elements of our food. For we already know that food is life, that it is the very principle of life and that the whole world has been created as food for man. We also know that to offer this food, this world, this life to God is the initial "eucharistic" function of man, his very fulfillment as man. We know that we were created as *celebrants* of the sacrament of life, of its transformation into life in God, communion with God. We know that real life is "eucharist," a movement of love and adoration toward God, the movement in which alone the meaning and the value of all that exists can be revealed and fulfilled. We know that we have lost this eucharistic life and, finally, we know that in Christ, the new Adam, the perfect man, this eucharistic life was restored to man. For he himself was the perfect Eucharist; He offered himself in total obedience, love and thanksgiving to God. God was his very life. And he gave this perfect and eucharistic life to us. In him God became our life.

And thus this offering to God of bread and wine, of the food that we must eat in order to live, is our offering to him of ourselves, of our life and of the whole world. "To take in our hands the whole world as if it were an apple!" said a

Russian poet. It is our Eucharist. It is the movement that
Adam failed to perform, and that in Christ has become the
very life of man. A movement of adoration and praise in
which all joy and suffering, all beauty and all frustration, all
hunger and all satisfaction are referred to their ultimate
End and become finally meaningful. Yes, to be sure, it is a
sacrifice: but sacrifice is the most natural act of man, the
very essence of his life. Man is a sacrificial being, because he
finds his life in love, and love is sacrificial: it puts the
"value," the very meaning of life in the other and gives life
to the other, and in this giving, in this sacrifice, finds the
meaning and joy of life.

We offer the world and ourselves to God. But we do it
in Christ and in remembrance of him. We do it in Christ
because he has already offered all that is to be offered to
God. He has performed once and for all this Eucharist and
nothing has been left unoffered. In him was Life—and this
Life of all of us, he gave to God. The Church is all those
who have been accepted into the eucharistic life of Christ.
And we do it in remembrance of him because, as we offer
again and again our life and our world to God, we discover
each time that there is nothing else to be offered but Christ
himself—the Life of the world, the fullness of all that
exists. It is his Eucharist, and he is the Eucharist. As the
prayer of offering says—"it is he who offers and it is he who
is offered." The liturgy has led us into the all-embracing
Eucharist of Christ, and has revealed to us that the only
Eucharist, the only offering of the world is Christ. We
come again and again with our lives to offer; we bring and

"sacrifice"—that is, give to God—what he has given us; and each time we come to the *End* of all sacrifices, of all offerings, of all eucharist, because each time it is revealed to us that Christ has *offered* all that exists, and that he and all that exists has been offered in his offering of himself. We are included in the Eucharist of Christ and Christ is our Eucharist.

And as the procession moves, it bears the bread and wine to the altar, and we know that it is Christ himself who takes all of us and the totality of our life to God in his eucharistic ascension. This is why at this moment of the liturgy we commemorate or remember. "Let the Lord God remember in his Kingdom. . . ." Remembrance is an act of *love*. God remembers us and his remembrance, his love is the foundation of the world. In Christ, we *remember*. We become again beings open to love, and we *remember*. The Church in its separation from "this world," on its journey to heaven *remembers* the world, remembers all men, remembers the whole of creation, takes it in love to God. The Eucharist is the sacrament of cosmic remembrance: it is indeed a restoration of love as the very life of the world.

8

The bread and wine are now on the altar, covered, hidden as our "life is hid with Christ in God" (Col 3:3). There lies, hidden in God, the totality of life, which Christ has brought back to God. And the celebrant says: "Let us love one another that in one accord we may confess. . . ." There

follows the kiss of peace, one of the fundamental acts of
Christian liturgy. The Church, if it is to be the Church,
must be the revelation of that divine Love which God
"poured out into our hearts." Without this love nothing is
"valid" in the Church because nothing is possible. The
content of Christ's Eucharist is Love, and only through
love can we enter into it and be made its partakers. Of this
love we are not capable. This love we have lost. This love
Christ has given us and this gift is the Church. The Church
constitutes itself through love and on love, and in this
world it is to "witness" to Love, to re-present it, to make
Love present. Love alone creates and transforms: it is, therefore, the very "principle" of the sacrament.

9

"Let us lift up our hearts," says the celebrant, and the people answer: "We have lifted them up to the Lord." The
Eucharist is an *anaphora*, the "lifting up" of our offering,
and, of ourselves. It is the ascension of the Church to
heaven. "But what do I care about heaven," says St. John
Chrysostom, "when I myself have become heaven. . . ."
The Eucharist has so often been explained with reference
to the gifts alone: What "happens" to bread and wine, and
why, and when does it happen! But we must understand
that what "happens" to bread and wine, happens *because*
something has, first of all, happened to us, to the Church.
It is because we have "constituted" the Church, and this
means we have followed Christ in his ascension; because he

has accepted us at his table in his Kingdom; because, in terms of theology, we have entered the Eschaton, and are now standing beyond time and space; it is because all this has first happened to us that something will happen to bread and wine.

"Let us lift up our hearts," says the celebrant.

"We lift them up unto the Lord," answers the congregation.

"Let us give thanks unto the Lord" (*Eucharistisomen*), then says the celebrant.

10

When man stands before the throne of God, when he has fulfilled all that God has given him to fulfill, when all sins are forgiven, all joy restored, then there is nothing else for him to do but to give thanks. Eucharist (thanksgiving) is the state of perfect man. Eucharist is the life of paradise. Eucharist is the only full and real response of man to God's creation, redemption and gift of heaven. But this perfect man who stands before God is *Christ*. In him alone all that God has given man was fulfilled and brought back to heaven. He alone is the perfect Eucharistic Being. He is the Eucharist of the world. In and through this Eucharist the whole creation becomes what it always was to be and yet failed to be.

"It is fitting and right to give thanks," answers the congregation, expressing in these words that "unconditional

surrender" with which true "religion" begins. For faith is
not the fruit of intellectual search, or of Pascal's "betting."
It is not a reasonable solution to the frustrations and anxieties of life. It does not arise out of a "lack" of something,
but finally, ultimately it comes out of fullness, love and joy.
"It is meet and right" expresses all this. It is the only possible response to the divine invitation to live and to receive
abundant life.

And so the priest begins the great Eucharistic Prayer:

It is meet and right that we should sing of Thee, bless Thee,
praise Thee, give thanks unto Thee, and adore Thee in all places
of Thy dominion. For Thou art God ineffable, incomprehensible, invisible, inconceivable; Thou art from everlasting and
art changeless. . . . Thou from nothingness has called us into
being, and when we had fallen away from Thee, Thou didst
raise us again. And Thou hast not ceased to do all things until
Thou hadst brought us back to heaven and endowed us with
Thy Kingdom which is to come. . . . For all these things we
give thanks unto Thee, for all the things whereof we know, and
those whereof we know not, for all the benefits bestowed upon
us, both the manifest and the unseen. . . .

This beginning of the Eucharistic Prayer is usually
termed the "Preface." And although this preface belongs to
all known eucharistic rites, not much attention was given
to it in the development of eucharistic theology. A
"preface" is something that does not really belong to the
body of a book. And theologians neglected it because they
were anxious to come to the real "problems": those of consecration, the change of the elements, sacrifice, and other
matters. It is here that we find the main "defect" of Chris-

tian theology; the theology of the Eucharist ceased to be eucharistic and thus took away the eucharistic spirit from the whole understanding of sacrament, from the very life of the Church. The long controversy about the words of institution and the invocation of the Holy Spirit (*epiclesis*) that went on for centuries between the East and the West is a very good example of this "noneucharistic" stage in the history of sacramental theology.

But we must understand that it is precisely this *preface* —this act, these words, this movement of thanksgiving— that really "makes possible" all that follows. For without this beginning the rest could not take place. The Eucharist of Christ and Christ the Eucharist is the "breakthrough" that brings us to the table in the Kingdom, raises us to heaven, and makes us partakers of the divine food. For eucharist—thanksgiving and praise—is the very form and content of the new life that God granted us when in Christ he reconciled us with himself. The reconciliation, the forgiveness, the power of life—all this has its purpose and fulfillment in this new state of being, this new style of life which is Eucharist, the only real life of creation with God and in God, the only true relationship between God and the world.

It is indeed the *preface* to the world to come, the door into the Kingdom: and this we confess and proclaim when, speaking of the Kingdom *which is to come*, we affirm that God *has already endowed us with it*. This future has been given to us in the past that it may constitute the very *present*, the life itself, now, of the Church.

11

And thus the preface fulfills itself in the Sanctus—the Holy, Holy, Holy of the eternal doxology, which is the secret essence of all that exists: "Heaven and earth are full of Thy glory." We had to ascend to heaven in Christ to see and to understand the creation in its real being as glorification of God, as that *response* to divine love in which alone creation becomes what God wants it to be: thanksgiving, eucharist, adoration. It is here—in the heavenly dimension of the Church, with "thousands of Archangels and myriads of Angels, with the Cherubim and Seraphim . . . who soar aloft, borne on their pinions . . ."—that we can finally "express ourself," and this expression is:

Holy, Holy, Holy,
Lord of Sabaoth.
Heaven and earth are full of thy glory.
Hosanna in the highest.
Blessed is He that cometh in the Name of the Lord.

This is the ultimate purpose of all that exists, the *end*, the goal and the fulfillment, because this is the *beginning*, the principle of Creation.

12

But as we stand before God, remember all that he has done for us, and offer to him our thanksgiving for all his benefits, we inescapably discover that the content of all this thanksgiving and remembrance is Christ. All remembrance is ultimately the remembrance of Christ, all thanksgiving is finally thanksgiving for Christ. "In Him was life and that life was the light of men." And in the light of the Eucharist we see that Christ is indeed the life and light of all that exists, and the glory that fills heaven and earth. There is nothing else to remember, nothing else to be thankful for, because in him everything finds its being, its life, its end.

And the Sanctus, therefore, brings us so simply, so logically to that one man, one night, one event in which this world found once for all its judgment and its salvation. It is not that having sung the Sanctus and confessed the majesty of divine glory, we put this aside and go into the next subdivision of the prayer, the Remembrance. No, the Remembrance is the fullness of our doxology, it is again the eucharist that "naturally" leads us into the very heart and content of all remembrance and thanksgiving.

Holy and most holy art Thou in Thy glorious majesty,
Who hast so loved the world
That Thou gavest Thine only-begotten Son,
That whosoever believeth on Him
Should not perish but have everlasting life,
Who, when He had come
And had performed all that was appointed for our sakes,
In the night on which he was given up, or
In which, rather, He did give Himself
For the life of the world,
Took bread in his holy and pure and sinless hands
And when He had given thanks, and blessed it, and sanctified it,
He gave it to His holy disciples, saying:
Take, eat, this is my Body which is broken for you
For the remission of sins.

And in like manner, after supper
He took the cup, saying:
Drink all ye of this: this is my Blood of the New Testament,
Which is shed for you, and for many
For the remission of sins.

As we stand before God, there is nothing else we can remember and bring with us and offer to God but this self offering of Christ, because in it all thanksgiving, all remembrance, all offering—that is, the whole life of man and of the world—were fulfilled. And so:

Remembering this commandment of salvation,
And all those things which for our sakes were brought to pass,
The Cross, the Grave, the Resurrection on the third day,
The Ascension into Heaven, the Sitting on the right hand,
The Second and glorious Advent—
Thine own of thine own we offer unto Thee,
In behalf of all and for all. . . .

13

Up to this point the Eucharist was our ascension in Christ, our entrance in him into the "world to come." And now, in this eucharistic offering in Christ of all things to the One to whom they belong and in whom alone they really exist —now this movement of ascension has reached its end. We are at the paschal table of the Kingdom. What we have offered—our food, our life, ourselves, and the whole world —we offered in Christ and as Christ because he himself has assumed our life and is our life. And now all this is given back to us as the gift of new life and therefore—necessarily —as food.

"This is my body, this is my blood. Take, eat, drink. . . ."
And generations upon generations of theologians ask the
same questions. How is this possible? How does this happen? And what exactly does happen in this transformation?
And when exactly? And what is the cause? No answer
seems to be satisfactory. Symbol? But what is a symbol?
Substance, accidents? Yet one immediately feels that something is lacking in all these theories, in which the Sacrament is reduced to the categories of time, substance, and
causality, the very categories of "this world."

Something is lacking because the theologian thinks of
the sacrament and forgets the liturgy. As a good scientist he
first isolates the object of his study, reduces it to one moment, to one "phenomenon"—and then, proceeding from
the general to the particular, from the known to the un-
known, he gives a definition, which in fact raises more questions than it answers. But throughout our study the main
point has been that the whole liturgy is sacramental, that is,
one transforming act and one ascending movement. And
the very goal of this movement of ascension is to take us
out of "this world" and to make us partakers of the world
to come. In this world—the one that condemned Christ
and by doing so has condemned itself—no bread, no wine
can become body and blood of Christ. Nothing which is a
part of it can be "sacralized." But the liturgy of the Church
is always an anaphora, a lifting up, an ascension. The
Church fulfills itself in heaven in that new eon which
Christ has inaugurated in his death, resurrection and ascension, and which was given to the Church on the day of

Pentecost as its life, as the "end" toward which it moves. In this world Christ is crucified, his body broken, and his blood shed. And we must go out of this world, we must ascend to heaven in Christ in order to become partakers of the world to come.

But this is not an "other" world, different from the one God has created and given to us. It is our same world, *already* perfected in Christ, but *not yet* in us. It is our same world redeemed and restored in which Christ "fills all things with Himself." And since God has created the world as food for us and has given us food as means of communion with him, as life in him—the new food of the new life which we receive from God in his Kingdom *is Christ himself.* He is our bread—because from the very beginning all our hunger was a hunger for him and all our bread was but a symbol of him, a symbol that had to become reality.

He became man and lived in this world. He ate and drank, and this means that the world of which he partook, our very food, became his body, his life. But his life was totally, absolutely *eucharistic*—all of it was transformed into communion with God and all of it ascended into heaven. And now he shares this glorified life with us. "What I have done alone—I give it now to you: take, eat. . . ."

We offered the bread in remembrance of Christ because we know that Christ is Life, and all food, therefore, must lead us to him. And now when we receive this bread from his hands, we know that he has taken up all life, filled it with himself, made it what it was meant to be: communion

with God, sacrament of his presence and love. There and
only there can we confess with St. Basil that "this bread is
in very truth the precious body of our Lord, this wine the
precious blood of Christ." What is "supernatural" here, in
this world, is revealed as "natural" there. And it is always in
order to lead us "there" and to make us what we are that
the Church fulfills itself in liturgy.

14

It is the Holy Spirit who *manifests* the bread as the body
and the wine as the blood of Christ.[1] The Orthodox
Church has always insisted that the *transformation* (*metab-
ole*) of the eucharistic elements is performed by the
epiclesis—the invocation of the Holy Spirit—and not by
the words of institution. This doctrine, however, was often
misunderstood by the Orthodox themselves. Its point is not
to replace one "causality"—the words of institution—by
another, a different "formula." It is to reveal the eschatological character of the sacrament. The Holy Spirit comes
on the "last and great day" of Pentecost. He manifests the
world to come. He inaugurates the Kingdom. He always
takes us *beyond*. To be in the Spirit means to be in heaven,
for the Kingdom of God is "joy and peace in the Holy
Spirit." And thus in the Eucharist it is he who *seals* and

---

[1] See the Liturgy of St. Basil: ". . . and manifest this bread as in
very truth the precious Body . . . this chalice as in very truth the
precious Blood. . . ."

confirms our ascension into heaven, who transforms the Church into the body of Christ and—therefore—manifests the elements of our offering as *communion in the Holy Spirit*. This is the consecration.

15

But before we can partake of the heavenly food there remains one last, essential and necessary act: the *intercession*. To be in Christ means to be like him, to make ours the very movement of his life. And as he "ever liveth to make intercession" for all "that come unto God by him" (Heb 7:25), so we cannot help accepting his intercession as our own. The Church is not a society for escape—corporately or individually—from this world to taste of the mystical bliss of eternity. Communion is not a "mystical experience": we drink of the chalice of Christ, and he gave himself for the life of the world. The bread on the paten and the wine in the chalice are to remind us of the incarnation of the Son of God, of the cross and death. And thus it is the very joy of the Kingdom that makes us *remember* the world and pray for it. It is the very communion with the Holy Spirit that enables us to love the world with the love of Christ. The Eucharist is the sacrament of unity and the *moment of truth:* here we see the world in Christ, as it really is, and not from our particular and therefore limited and partial points of view. Intercession begins here, in the glory of the messianic banquet, and this is the only true beginning for the Church's mission. It is when, "having put aside all earthly care," we seem to have left *this world*, that we, in fact, recover it in all its reality.

Intercession constitutes, thus, the only real preparation for communion. For in and through communion not only do we become one body and one spirit, but we are restored to that solidarity and love, which the world has lost. And the great Eucharistic Prayer is now summed up in the Lord's Prayer, each petition of which implies the total and complete dedication to God's Kingdom in the world. It is *his* prayer, and he *gave* it to us, made it our prayer, as he made his Father *our* Father. No one has been "worthy" to receive communion, no one has been *prepared* for it. At this point all merits, all righteousness, all devotions, disappear and dissolve. Life comes again to us as *Gift*, a free and divine gift. This is why in the Orthodox Church we call the eucharistic elements Holy Gifts. Adam is again introduced into Paradise, taken out of nothingness and crowned king of creation. Everything is free, nothing is due and yet all is given. And, therefore, the greatest humility and obedience is to *accept* the gift, to say yes—in joy and gratitude. There is nothing we can *do*, yet we become all that God wanted us to be from eternity, when we are *eucharistic*.

16

And now the time has come for us to *return into the world*. "Let us depart in peace," says the celebrant as he leaves the altar, and this is the last *commandment* of the liturgy. We must not stay on Mount Tabor, although we know that it is good for us to be there. We are sent back. But now—"we have seen the true Light, we have partaken of the Holy Spirit." And it is as witnesses of this Light, as witnesses of the Spirit, that we must "go forth" and begin the never-ending mission of the Church. Eucharist was the *end* of the journey, the end of time. And now it is again the *beginning*, and things that were impossible are again revealed to us as possible. The time of the world has become the time of the Church, the time of salvation and redemption. And God has made us *competent*, as Paul Claudel has said; competent to be his witnesses, to fulfill what he has done and is ever doing. This is the meaning of the Eucharist; this is why the mission of the Church begins in the liturgy of ascension, for it alone makes possible the liturgy of mission.

3 THE TIME OF MISSION

As we leave the church after the Sunday Eucharist we enter again into time, and time, therefore, is the first "object" of our Christian faith and action. For it is indeed the icon of our fundamental reality, of the optimism as well as of the pessimism of our life, of life as life and of life as death. Through time on the one hand we experience life as a possibility, growth, fulfillment, as a movement toward a future. Through time, on the other hand, all future is dissolved in death and annihilation. Time is the only reality of life, yet it is a strangely nonexistent reality: it constantly dissolves life in a past which no longer is, and in a future which always leads to death. By itself time is nothing but a line of telegraph poles strung out into the distance and at some point along the way is our death.

All generations, all philosophers have always been aware of this anxiety of time, of its paradox. All philosophy, all religion is ultimately an attempt to solve the "problem of time." And thousands of books, Christian and non-Christian, have been written about it. It is not our purpose, however, to add another "theology of time" to all those that exist already. It is rather to describe very briefly the experience of time, which Christians have had from the very beginning and which is still given, offered to them in the Church. Here again, what the Church offers is not a "solution" of a philosophical problem, but a *gift*. And it becomes solution only as it is accepted as freely and joyfully as it is given. Or, it may be, the joy of that gift makes both the problem and the solution unnecessary, irrelevant.

2

To understand the gift, we shall once more turn to the liturgy, decipher again its forgotten language. Today no one, except the peculiar and esoteric race of men called "liturgiologists," is interested in what was in the past a major preoccupation for Christians: the feasts and the seasons, the cycles of prayer, a very real concern about the "*kairos*"—the time of liturgical celebration. Not only the average layman, even the theologian seems to say: the world of Christian "symbolism" is no longer our world, all this failed, all this is gone and we have more serious affairs to attend to; it would be unthinkable, ridiculous to try to solve any real "problem" of modern life by referring it, say, to Easter or Pentecost, or even to Sunday.

Yet at this point let us ask a few questions. Are these "symbols" merely "symbolic"? Or is their failure perhaps to be explained precisely by the symbolic value attached to them by Christians themselves, who ceased to understand their true nature? And did they not cease to understand this nature because at one time (it would take too long to elaborate on this here) Christians came to think that "religion" has nothing to do with time, is in fact salvation from time? Before we gain the right to dispose of the old "symbols" we must understand that the real tragedy of Christianity is not its "compromise" with the world and progressive "materialism," but on the contrary, its "spiritualization" and transformation into "religion." And religion—as we know already—has thus come to mean a world of pure spirituality, a concentration of attention on matters pertaining to the "soul." Christians were tempted to reject time altogether and replace it with mysticism and "spiritual" pursuits, to live as Christians out of time and thereby escape its frustrations; to insist that time has no real meaning from the point of view of the Kingdom which is "beyond time." And they finally succeeded. They left time meaningless indeed, although full of Christian "symbols." And today they themselves do not know what to do with these symbols. For it is impossible to "put Christ back into Christmas" if he has not redeemed—that is, made meaningful—time itself.

We must understand, therefore, that the intensive, almost pathological, preoccupation of our modern world with time and its "problem" is rooted in this specifically Christian failure. It is because of us, Christians, that the world in which we live has literally *no time*. Is it not true that the more "time-saving" devices we invent, the less time we have? The joyless *rush* is interrupted by *relaxation* ("sit back and relax!"), but such is the horror of the strange vacuum covered by this truly demonic word, "revelation," that men must take pills to endure it, and buy expensive books about how to *kill* this no man's land of "modern living."

There is *no time* because Christianity, on the one hand, made it impossible for man to live in the old natural time, broke beyond repair the cycle of the eternal return. It has announced the fullness of time, revealed time as history and fulfillment, and has truly poisoned us once for all with the dream of a meaningful time. There is no time, on the other hand, because having announced all this, Christianity abandoned time, invited Christians simply to leave it and to think of eternity as of an eternal rest (if not yet "relaxation"). To be sure, one can still adorn the meaningless time with beautiful symbols and "colorful rites," preferably "ancient." One can—at regular intervals and by consulting the "rubrics"—change the colors of liturgical vestments, and spice the same eternal sermon with some references to Easter, or Christmas, or Epiphany. All this, "inspiring" and "uplifting" as it may be, has no meaning for the real time in which the real man must live, or rather, for the absence of time, which makes his life a nightmarish alternation of "rush" and "relaxation."

And thus our question is: did Christ, the Son of God, rise from the dead on the *first* day of the week, did he send his Spirit on the day of *Pentecost*, did he, in other words, *enter time* that we may only "symbolize" it in fine celebrations which, although connected with the days and the hours, have no power to give time a real meaning, to transform and redeem it?

3

From the beginning Christians had their own day, and it is
in its peculiar nature that we find the key to the Christian
experience of time. To recover it, however, we must go
beyond Constantine's legislation which, by instituting Sunday as the compulsory, weekly day of rest, made it the
Christian substitute for the Jewish Sabbath. After that the
unique and paradoxical significance of the Lord's Day was
little by little forgotten. And yet its significance came precisely from its relation to the Sabbath, that is, to the whole
biblical understanding of time. In the Jewish worldview
and religious experience Sabbath, the seventh day has a
tremendous importance: it is the participation by man in,
and his affirmation of, the goodness of God's creation.
"And God saw it was good. . . . And God blessed the
seventh day, and sanctified it: because in it he had rested
from all his work which God created and made" (Gn 1:25,
2:3). The seventh day is thus the joyful acceptance of the
world created by God, as good. The rest prescribed on that
day, and which was somehow obscured later by petty and
legalistic prescriptions and taboos, is not at all our modern
"relaxation," an absence of work. It is the active participation in the "Sabbath delight," in the sacredness and fullness of divine peace, as the fruit of all work, as the crowning of all time. It has thus both cosmic and eschatological
connotations.

Yet this "good" world, which the Jew blesses on the

seventh day, is at the same time the world of sin and revolt
against God, and its time is the time of man's exile and
alienation from God. And, therefore, the seventh day points
beyond itself toward a new Lord's Day—the day of salvation and redemption, of God's triumph over his enemies.
In the late Jewish apocalyptic writings there emerges the
idea of a new day which is both the *eighth*—because it is
beyond the frustrations and limitations of "seven," the time
of *this* world—and the *first*, because with it begins the new
time, that of the Kingdom. It is from this idea that grew
the Christian Sunday.

Christ rose from the dead on the *first day* after Sabbath.
The life that shone forth from the grave was beyond the
inescapable limitations of "seven," of time that leads to
death. It was thus the beginning of a new life and of a new
time. It was truly the eighth and the first day and it became
the day of the Church. The risen Christ, according to the
fourth Gospel, appeared to his disciples on the first day
(Jn 20:19) and then "after eight days" (20:26). This is
the day on which the Church celebrates the Eucharist—the
sacrament of its ascension to the Kingdom and of its
participation at the messianic banquet in the "age to come"
—on which the Church fulfills itself as new life. The ear-
liest documents mention that Christians meet *statu die*—
on a fixed day—and nothing in the long history of Christianity could alter the importance of this fixed day.

A "fixed day." . . . If Christianity were a purely "spiritual" and eschatological faith there would have been no
need for a "fixed day," because mysticism has no interest in

time. To save one's soul one needs, indeed, no "calendar."
And if Christianity were but a new "religion," it would
have established its calendar, with the usual opposition between the "holy days" and the "profane days"—those to be
"kept" and "observed" and those religiously insignificant.
Both understandings did in fact appear later. But this was
not at all the original meaning of the "fixed day." It was
not meant to be a "holy day" opposed to profane ones, a
commemoration in time of a past event. Its true meaning
was in the transformation of time, not of calendar. For, on
the one hand, Sunday remained *one of the days* (for more
than three centuries it was not even a day of rest), the first
of the week, fully belonging to *this* world. Yet on the other
hand, on that day, through the eucharistic ascension, the
day of the Lord was revealed and manifested in all its glory
and transforming power, as the *end* of this world, as the *beginning* of the world to come. And thus through that one
day, all days, all time were transformed into times of *remembrance and expectation*. Remembrance of this ascension, for "we have seen the true light . . . ," expectation
of its *coming*. All days, all hours were now referred to this
end of all "natural" life, to the *beginning* of the new life.
The week was no longer a sequence of "profane" days, with
rest on the "sacred" day at their end. It was now a movement from Mount Tabor into the world, from the world
into the "day without evening" of the world to come.
Every day, every hour acquired now an importance, a
gravity it could not have had before: each day was now to
be a *step* in this movement, a moment of decision and wit-

ness, a time of ultimate meaning. Sunday thus was not a "sacred" day—to be "observed" or "kept" apart from all other days, opposed to them. It did not interrupt time with a "timeless" mystical ecstasy. It was not a "break" in an otherwise meaningless sequence of days and nights. By remaining one of the ordinary days, and yet by revealing itself through the Eucharist as the eighth and first day, it gave all days their true meaning. It made the time of this world a time of the *end*, and it made it also the time of the *beginning*.

4

We must turn now to the second dimension of the Christian experience of time—to the so-called "Christian year." To speak of it, however, is even more difficult than to speak of Sunday, because for the modern Christian the relation between this "Christian year" and time has become incomprehensible and, therefore, irrelevant. On certain dates the Church commemorates certain events of the past —nativity, resurrection, the descent of the Holy Spirit. These dates are an occasion for a liturgical "illustration" of certain theological affirmations, but as such they are in no way related to the real time or of consequence for it. Even within the Church itself they are mere "breaks" in the normal routine of its activities, and many business minded and action-oriented Christians secretly consider these festivals and celebrations a waste of time. And if other

Christians welcome them as additional days of rest and "vacation," no one seriously thinks of them as the very heart of the Church's life and mission. There exists, in other words, a serious crisis in the very idea of a feast and it is here that we must begin our brief discussion of the Christian year.

Feast means *joy*. Yet, if there is something that we—the serious, adult and frustrated Christians of the twentieth century—look at with suspicion, it is certainly joy. How can one be joyful when so many people suffer? When so many things are to be done? How can one indulge in festivals and celebrations when people expect from us "serious" answers to their problems? Consciously or subconsciously Christians have accepted the whole ethos of our joyless and business-minded culture. They believe that the only way to be taken "seriously" by the "serious"—that is, by modern man—is to be serious, and, therefore, to reduce to a symbolic "minimum" what in the past was so tremendously central in the life of the Church—the joy of a feast. The modern world has relegated joy to the category of "fun" and "relaxation." It is justified and permissible on our "time off"; it is a concession, a compromise. And Christians have come to believe all this, or rather they have ceased to believe that the feast, the joy have something to do precisely with the "serious problems" of life itself, may even be *the* Christian answer to them. With all these spiritual and cultural connotations, the "Christian year"—the sequence of liturgical commemorations and celebrations—ceased to be the generator of power and is now looked upon as a more

or less antiquated decoration of religion. It is used as a kind
of "audio-visual" aid in religious education, but it is neither
a root of Christian life and action, nor a "goal" toward
which they are oriented.

To understand the true nature—and "function"—of
feasts we must remember that Christianity was born and
preached at first in cultures in which feasts and celebrations
were an organic and essential part of the whole worldview
and way of life. For the man of the past a feast was not
something accidental and "additional": it was his way of
putting *meaning* into his life, of liberating it from the
animal rhythm of work and rest. A feast was not a simple
"break" in the otherwise meaningless and hard life of work,
but a justification of that work, its fruit, its—so to speak—
sacramental transformation into joy and, therefore, into
freedom. A feast was thus always deeply and organically related to time, to the natural cycles of time, to the whole
framework of man's life in the world. And, whether we
want it or not, whether we like it or not, Christianity *accepted* and made its own this fundamentally human phenomenon of feast, as it accepted and made its own the
whole man and all his needs. But, as in everything else,
Christians accepted the feast not only by giving it a new
meaning, by transforming its "content," but by taking it,
along with the whole of "natural" man, through death and
resurrection.

Yes, as we have already said, Christianity was on the one
hand the end of all natural joy. It revealed its impossibility,
its futility, its sadness—because by revealing the perfect

man it revealed the abyss of man's alienation from God and the inexhaustible sadness of this alienation. The cross of Christ signified an end of all "natural" rejoicing, made it, indeed, impossible. From this point of view the sad "seriousness" of modern man is certainly of Christian origin, even if this has been forgotten by that man himself. Since the Gospel was preached in this world, all attempts to go back to a pure "pagan joy," all "renaissances," all "healthy optimism" were bound to fail. "There is but one sadness," said Léon Bloy, "that of not being a saint." And it is this sadness that permeates mysteriously the whole life of the world, its frantic and pathetic hunger and thirst for perfection, which kills all joy. Christianity made it impossible simply to rejoice in the natural cycles—in harvests and new moons. Because it relegated the perfection of joy to the inaccessible future—as the goal and end of all work—it made all human life an "effort"—a "work."

Yet, on the other hand Christianity was the revelation and the gift of joy, and thus, the gift of genuine *feast*. Every Saturday night at the resurrection vigil we sing, "for, through the Cross, there came joy to the whole world." This joy is pure joy because it does not depend on anything in this world, is not the reward of anything in us. It is totally and absolutely a *gift*, the *"charis,"* the grace. And being pure gift, this joy has a transforming power, *the only really transforming power in this world.* It is the "seal" of the Holy Spirit on the life of the Church—on its faith, hope and love.

5

Through the Cross joy came to the whole world . . ."—
and not just to some men as their personal and private joy.
Once more, were Christianity pure "mysticism," pure "eschatology," there would be no need for feasts and celebrations. A holy soul would keep its secret feast apart from the
world, to the extent that it could free itself from its time.
But joy was given to the Church for the world—that the
Church might be a witness to it and transform the world
by joy. Such is the "function" of Christian feasts and the
meaning of their belonging to time.

For us today Easter and Pentecost—to limit ourselves to
the two initial and fundamental feasts which give its true
significance to the Christian year—are primarily the annual
commemorations of two events of the past: Christ's resurrection and the descent of the Holy Spirit. But what is
"commemoration"? Is not the whole life of the Church a
constant remembrance of the death and resurrection of
Christ? Is not its whole life called to be the manifestation
of the Holy Spirit? In the Orthodox Church, each Sunday
is the day of resurrection and each Eucharist a Pentecost.
In fact, the understanding of feasts as historical commemorations which emerged little by little after Constantine meant a transformation of their initial meaning and,
strange as it may seem, divorced them from their living
connection with the real time. Thus in Australia today
Easter is celebrated in the fall and no one seems to find it

odd, because for several centuries the Christian calendar
was understood as a system of *holy days* to be observed
within time, that is, among "profane" days, but without
any special relation to them.

But if the early Church adopted or, rather, simply kept
as its own, the great Jewish festivals of Passover and Pentecost, it was not because they reminded it of Christ's resurrection and the coming of the Spirit (its remembrance was
the very essence of the Church's whole life)—but because
they were, even before Christ, the announcement, the anticipation of that experience of time and of life in time, of
which the Church was the manifestation and the fulfillment. They were—to use another image—the "material" of
a *sacrament of time* to be performed by the Church. We
know that both feasts originated as the annual celebration
of spring and of the first fruits of nature. In this respect
they were the very expression of feast as man's *joy about
life*. They celebrated the world coming back to life again
after the death of winter, becoming again the food and life
of man. And it is very significant that this most "natural,"
all-embracing and universal feast—that of life itself—became the starting point, and indeed the foundation of the
long transformation of the idea and experience of feast. It
is equally significant that in this transformation each new
stage did not abolish and simply replace the previous one,
but fulfilled it in an even deeper and greater meaning until
the whole process was consummated in Christ himself. The
mystery of the *natural* time, the bondage to winter and release in spring, was fulfilled in the mystery of time as

history—the bondage to Egypt and the release into the Promised Land. And the mystery of the historical time was transformed into the mystery of the eschatological time, of its understanding as *passover*—the "passage" into the ultimate joy of salvation and redemption, as movement toward the fulfillment of the Kingdom. And when Christ— "our Passover" (1 Cor 5:7) performed his *passage* to the Father, he assumed and fulfilled all these meanings—the whole movement of time in all its dimensions; and on the "last and great day of Pentecost" he inaugurated the new time, the new "eon" of the Spirit.

And thus Easter is not a commemoration of an event, but—every year—the fulfillment of time itself, of our real time. For we still live in the same three dimensions of time: in the world of nature, in the world of history, in the world of expectation. And in each one of them man is in a secret search for joy, that is, for an ultimate meaning and perfection, for an ultimate fulfillment which he does not find. Time always points to a feast, to a joy, which by itself it cannot give or realize. So needful of *meaning*, time becomes the very form and image of meaninglessness.

But on Easter night the meaning is given. And it is not given by means of "explanation" or even "commemoration," but as a gift of joy itself, the joy of participation in the new time of the Kingdom. To experience this, one has to enter into an Orthodox Church on Easter night, after the procession has gone around the church, has stopped in the darkness at the closed door. And now the doors are opened with the announcement: "Christ is risen!" The paschal celebration has begun. What is this night of which St. Gregory of Nyssa says that it becomes brighter than the day and which the Orthodox call the "bright night"? One could describe the various rites, one could analyze the texts, one could mention a thousand details, but in the last count, all this is secondary. The only reality is joy and this joy is given.

> Enter ye all into the joy of your Lord,
> You who are rich and you the poor, come to the feast,
> Receive all the riches of loving-kindness . . .
> And let no one bewail his poverty,
> *For the universal Kingdom has been revealed.*

And the whole service is nothing but a response to this joy, its acceptance, its celebration, the affirmation of its reality.

> The *Pascha* (passover) of the Lord,
> From death unto life,
> And from earth unto heaven
> Has Christ our God brought us over . . .
>
> Now are all things filled with light,
> Heaven and earth and the places under the earth.
> All Creation does celebrate the Resurrection of Christ
> On whom it is founded . . .
>
> We celebrate the death of Death,
> The annihilation of Hell,
> The beginning of a life new and everlasting.
> And with ecstasy we sing praises to the author thereof . . .
>
> This is the chosen and holy Day,
> The one King and Lord of Sabbaths,
> The Feast of Feasts and the Triumph of Triumphs . . .

O Christ, the Passover great and most holy!
O Wisdom, Word and Power of God!
Grant that we may more perfectly partake of Thee
In the day of Thy Kingdom which knoweth no night.

We called Easter the "sacrament of time." Indeed, the joy given on that night, the light that transforms the night into a night "brighter than day" are to become the secret joy and the ultimate meaning of all time, and thus *transform* the year into a "Christian year." After the Easter night comes the morning, and then another night and another new day. Time begins again, but it is now filled from "inside" with that unique and truly "eschatological" experience of joy. A ray of sun on a gloomy factory wall, the smile on a human face, each rainy morning, the fatigue of each evening—all is now referred to this joy and can, not only point beyond itself, but also be a sign, a mark, a secret "presence" of that joy.

For fifty days after Easter it is granted to us to live in the paschal joy, to experience time as the *feast*. And then comes the "last and great" day of Pentecost and with it our *return* into the real time of this world. At Vespers of that day the Christians are ordered—for the first time since Easter—*to kneel*. The night is approaching, the night of time and history, of the daily effort, of the fatigue and temptations, of the whole inescapable burden of life. The Easter season is at its end—but as we enter the night, we know that the end has been transformed into a beginning, that all time is now the time *after Pentecost*. (That is why we number all Sundays from this point until the next Easter season.) This is

the time in which the joy of the Kingdom, the "peace and
joy" of the Holy Spirit are at work. "There shall be no separation, O friends! said Christ. . . ."

The time itself is now measured by the rhythm of the
end and the beginning, of the end transformed into beginning, of the beginning announcing the fulfillment. The
Church is *in time* and its life in this world is *fasting*, that
is, a life of effort, sacrifice, self-denial and dying. The
Church's very mission is to become all things to all men.
But how could the Church fulfill this mission, how could
it be the salvation of the world, if it were not, first of all and
above everything else, the divine gift of Joy, the fragrance
of the Holy Spirit, the presence here in time of the feast of
the Kingdom?

6

After the week and the year—the day: the most direct and
immediate unit of time. It is here, in the reality of daily life,
that the theology of time, expressed in the experience of
Sunday and Easter, must find its application. We realize, of
course, that the daily cycle of services, abandoned long ago,
is not very likely to be restored. Yet, what *is* to be restored,
or rather, rediscovered, is the relation of the Church and of
the individual Christian to the time of the day, relation
which was (and theoretically still is) the theme, the content of the daily services. For these were not meant to be
"prayer breaks," periods of spiritual refreshment and "peace
of mind," but truly *liturgical acts*, that is, acts performed on

behalf of and for the whole community, as an essential part of the redeeming mission of the Church.

Contrary to our secular experience of time, the liturgical day begins with Vespers, and this means, in the evening. This is, of course, the reminiscence of the biblical "And the evening and the morning were the first day" (Gn 1:5). Yet it is more than a reminiscence. For it is, indeed, the end of each "unit" of time that reveals its pattern and meaning, that gives to time its reality. Time is always growth, but only at the end can we discern the direction of that growth and see its fruits. It is at the end, in the evening of each day that God sees his creation as good; it is at the end of creation that he gives it to man. And thus, it is at the end of the day that the Church begins the liturgy of time's sanctification.

We come to church, we who are in the world having lived through many hours and these hours filled, as usual, with work and rest, suffering and joy, hatred and love. Men died and men were born. For some it was the happiest day of their life, a day to be remembered forever. And for some others it brought the end of all their hopes, the destruction of their very soul. And the whole day is now here—unique, irreversible, irreparable. It is gone, but its results, its fruits will shape the next day, for what we have done once, remains forever.

But the vesperal service does not begin as a religious "epilogue" of the day, as a prayer added to all its other experience. It begins at the beginning, and this means in the "rediscovery," in adoration and thanksgiving, of the world

as God's creation. The Church takes us, as it were, to that
first evening on which man, called by God to life, opened
his eyes and saw what God in his love was giving to him,
saw all the beauty, all the glory of the temple in which he
was standing, and rendered thanks to God. And in this
thanksgiving he *became himself.*

> Praise the Lord, O my soul. Blessed art Thou O Lord . . .
> O Lord, how manifold are thy works. In wisdom hast Thou
>   made them all.
> The earth is full of Thy riches.
> I will sing unto the Lord as long as I live
> I will praise my God, while I have my being (Ps 104).

And it must be so. There must be someone in this world
—which rejected God and in this rejection, in this blas-
phemy, became a chaos of darkness—there must be someone to stand in its center, and to discern, to see it again as
full of divine riches, as the cup, full of life and joy, as
beauty and wisdom, and to thank God for it. This "someone" is Christ, the new Adam who restores that "eucharistic life" which I, the old Adam, have rejected and lost; who
makes me again what I am, and restores the world to me.
And if the Church is *in Christ*, its initial act is always this
act of thanksgiving, of returning the world to God.

By contrast to the beauty and wonder of creation, however, the darkness and failure of the world is discovered, and
this is the second great theme of vespers. If Psalm 104
speaks truly, the world as we know it is—by contrast—a
nightmare. Because we have first seen the beauty of the
world, we can now see the ugliness, realize what we have

lost, understand how our whole life (and not only some "trespasses") has become sin, and can *repent* for it. The lights are now extinguished. The "royal doors" of the sanctuary are closed. The celebrant has put off his vestments; it is the naked and suffering man, who cries outside of Paradise, who in full awareness of his exile, of his betrayal, of his darkness, says to God: "Out of the deep have I cried unto Thee, O Lord." In the face of the glory of creation, there must be a tremendous sadness. God has given us another day, and we can see just how we have destroyed this gift of his. We are not "nice" Christians come apart from the ugly world. If we do not stand precisely as representatives of this world, as indeed the world itself, if we do not bear the whole burden of *this* day, our "piety" may still be pious. It is not Christian.

Now comes the third theme of Vespers: *redemption*. Into this world of sin and darkness light has come: "The gladsome radiance of the holy glory of the Father, immortal, heavenly, holy, blessed, Jesus Christ." The world is at its evening because the One bringing the final meaning to the world has come; in the darkness of this world, the light of Christ reveals again the true nature of things. This is not the world it was before Christ came: his coming now *belongs* to the world. The decisive event of the cosmos has taken place. We know now that the event of Christ must transform everything to do with our lives. It was only because of Christ that we had the heart to glory in the creation at the beginning of Vespers, only because he gave us the eyes to "behold God's gracious hand in all his works."

Now in the time in which we can thank God for Christ, we begin to understand that everything is transformed in Christ into its true wonder. In the radiance of his light the world is not commonplace. The very floor we stand on is a miracle of atoms whizzing about in space. The darkness of sin is clarified, and its burden shouldered. Death is robbed of its finality, trampled down by Christ's death. In a world where everything that seems to be present is immediately past, all is in Christ able to participate in the eternal present of God. This very evening is the real time of our life.

And thus we are brought to the last theme of vespers: that of the *end*. It is announced by the singing of the *Nunc Dimittis*. The words are attributed in the Gospel to the old man Simeon who had spent his life in constant expectation of the coming Messiah, because he had been told in a vision that he would not die before he saw the promised one of Israel. When Mary and Joseph brought the child Jesus to be presented to God in the temple, he was there and received him into his arms, and the Gospel records that he said:

Lord, now lettest Thou thy servant depart in peace, according to thy word. For mine eyes have seen thy Salvation, which Thou hast prepared before the face of all people; to be a light to lighten the Gentiles, and to be the glory of thy people Israel.

Simeon had been waiting all his life, and then at last the Christ Child was given to him: he held the Life of the world in his arms. He stood for the whole world in its expectation and longing, and the words he used to express his thanksgiving have become our own. He could recognize the Lord because he had expected him; he took him into his arms because it is natural to take someone you love into your arms; and then his life of waiting was fulfilled. He had beheld the One he had longed for. He had completed his purpose in life, and he was ready to die.

But death to him was no catastrophe. It was only a natural expression of the fulfillment of his waiting. He was not closing his eyes to the light he had at last seen; his death was only the beginning of more inward vision of that light. In the same way Vespers is the recognition that the evening of this world has come, which announces that day that has no evening. In this world, every day faces night; the world itself is facing night. It cannot last forever. Yet the Church is affirming that an evening is not only an end, but also a beginning, just as any evening is also the beginning of another day. In Christ and through Christ it may become the beginning of a new life, of the day that has no evening. For our eyes have seen salvation and a light which will never fail. And because of this, the time of this world is now pregnant with new life. We come into the presence of Christ to offer him our time, we extend our arms to receive him. And he fills this time with himself, He heals it and makes it—again and again—the time of salvation.

7

And the evening and the morning. . . ." When we first wake up, the initial sensation is always that of night, not of illumination; we are at our weakest, at our most helpless. It is like a man's first real experience of life in all its absurdity and solitude, at first kept from him by family warmth. We discover every morning in the amorphous darkness the inertia of life. And thus, the first theme of matins is again the coming of light into darkness. It begins, not like Vespers with the creation, but with the Fall. Yet in this very helplessness and despair, there is a hidden expectation, a thirst and hunger. And within this scene the Church declares its joy, not only against the grain of natural life, but fulfilling it. The Church announces every morning that God is the Lord, and it begins to organize life around God.

In the church the first lights of Matins are candles, as a foretaste of the sun. Then the sun itself rises, dispelling the darkness of the world, and in this the Church sees the rising of the true Light of the world, the Son of God. We know that our Redeemer lives, and that in the midst of the absurdity of life, he will be again revealed to us. Though the misfortunes of life "compass us about," yet each morning we can proclaim with the rising sun the coming of the long-expected Messiah. Despite everything, "this is the day which the Lord has made—we will rejoice and be glad in it. Blessed is He that cometh in the Name of the Lord."

As the light grows, the service refers the new morning to the new time. As Vespers referred evening to the whole Christian experience of the world as "evening"—so Matins refers morning to the Christian experience of the Church as "morning" and beginning.

These two complementary, yet absolutely essential, *dimensions* of time shape our life in time and, by giving time a new meaning, transform it into *Christian time*. This double experience is, indeed, to be applied to everything we have to do. We are always *between* morning and evening, *between* Sunday and Sunday, *between* Easter and Easter, *between* the two comings of Christ. The experience of time as *end* gives an absolute importance to whatever we do *now*, makes it final, decisive. The experience of time as *beginning* fills all our time with joy, for it adds to it the "coefficient" of eternity. "I shall not die but live and declare the works of the Lord." We are at work in the world, and this work —in fact, any work—if analyzed in terms of the world in itself, becomes meaningless, futile, irrelevant. In every city in the world there is each morning a rush of clean and shaven people getting to work. And every evening there is a rush of the same people, now tired and dirty, going in the opposite direction. But long, long ago a wise man looked at this rush (its forms change, but not its meaninglessness) and said:

Vanity of vanities. All is vanity.
What profit hath man of all his labor which he taketh under the sun?
One generation passeth away and another generation cometh;
But the earth abideth forever.
The eye is not satisfied with seeing, nor the ear filled with hearing.
There is no new thing under the sun. . . . (Eccl 1)

And this remains true of the *fallen* world. But we Christians have too often forgotten that God has redeemed the world. For centuries we have preached to the hurrying people: your daily rush has no meaning, yet, accept it—and you will be rewarded in *another* world by an eternal rest. But God revealed and offers us eternal Life and not eternal rest. And God revealed this eternal Life in the midst of time—and of its *rush*—as its secret meaning and goal. And thus he made time, and our work in it, into the *sacrament of the world to come*, the liturgy of fulfillment and ascension. It is when we have reached the very end of the world's self-sufficiency, that it *begins* again for us as the material of the sacrament that we are to fulfill in Christ.

"There is no new thing under the sun." Yet every day, every minute resounds now with the victorious affirmation: "Behold, I make all things new. I am Alpha and Omega, the beginning and the end . . ." (Rev 21:5–6).

All that we have said about time and its transformation and renewal has simply no meaning if there is no new man to perform the sacrament of time. It is of him that we must speak now and of the act in which the newness of life and the power to live by it are given him. We began, however, not at baptism, which is the beginning of Christian life, but with the Eucharist and time, because it was essential to establish the cosmic dimensions of the life given in baptism. For a long time the theological and spiritual interest in baptism was virtually disconnected from its cosmic significance, from the totality of man's relation to the world. It was explained as man's liberation from "original sin." But both original sin and the liberation from it were given an extremely narrow and individual meaning. Baptism was understood as the means to assure the individual salvation of man's soul. No wonder that such an understanding of baptism led to a similar narrowing of the baptismal liturgy. From an act of the whole Church, involving the whole cosmos, it became a private ceremony, performed in a corner of the church, by "private appointment," and in which the Church was reduced to the "minister of sacraments" and the cosmos to the three symbolic drops of water, considered as "necessary and sufficient" for the "validity" of the sacrament. *Validity* was the preoccupation—and not fullness, meaning, joy. Because of the obsession of baptismal theology with juridical and not ontological terms, the real question—*what* is made valid?—often remained unanswered.

Lately, it is true, there has occurred throughout the Christian world a certain widening of the theology of baptism. There has been a rediscovery of the meaning of baptism as entrance into, and integration in, the Church, of its "ecclesiological" significance. But ecclesiology, unless it is given its true cosmic perspective ("for the life of the world"), unless it is understood as the Christian form of "cosmology," is always becoming ecclesiolatry, making of the Church a "being in itself" and not the new relation of God, man and the world. And it is not "ecclesiology" that gives baptism its true meaning; it is rather in and through baptism that we find the first and fundamental meaning of the Church.

And baptism, by its very form and elements—the water of the baptismal font, the oil of christmation—refers us inescapably to "matter," to the world, to the cosmos. In the early Church the celebration of baptism took place during the solemn Easter vigil, and in fact, the Easter liturgy grew out of the "paschal mystery" of baptism. This means that baptism was understood as having a direct meaning for the "new time," of which Easter is the celebration and the manifestation, and that it was also referred to ordinary time. And finally, baptism and chrismation were always fulfilled in the Eucharist—which is the sacrament of the Church's ascension to the Kingdom, the sacrament of the "world to come."

I have already said that the tragedy of a certain theology (and piety) was that in its search for precise definitions, it artificially isolated the sacraments from the liturgy in which they were performed. The liturgy was relegated to the category of secondary, decorative and ritual elements having no bearing on the "esse" of the sacrament. By doing so, however, theology lost much of the true understanding of the sacramental reality. Baptism in particular has suffered an almost disastrous loss of meaning. And we must, therefore —in order to recover it—return to the "leitourgia" of the Church.

2

In the past, preparation for baptism sometimes lasted as long as three years. Now, however, that infant baptism has become virtually universal, this preparation is merely of historical interest. And yet it is important for us to remember that a great part of the Church's life was devoted to the preparation for baptism of the catechumens, those who already believed in Christ and were now on their way to the fulfillment of that faith in baptism. In the Orthodox Church, even today, the entire first part of the Eucharist is called the "Liturgy of the Catechumen." The liturgical seasons of Lent and Advent, the cycles of Christmas and Epiphany, the structure of Holy Week and, finally, the "solemnity of solemnities"—the Easter vigil—were all shaped in their development by the preparation for baptism and its celebration. The meaning of all this for us today is, first, that the whole life of the Church is, in a way, the explication and the manifestation of baptism, and second, that baptism forms the real content, the "existential" root of what we call now "religious education." The latter is not an abstract "knowledge about God" but the revelation of the wonderful things that have "happened" and happen to us in the divine gift of the new life.

The actual baptismal service as it is celebrated in the Orthodox Church begins with what was in the past the final act of the "catechumenate": the exorcisms, the renunciation of Satan and the confession of faith.

According to some modern interpreters of Christianity, "demonology" belongs to an antiquated worldview and cannot be taken seriously by the man who "uses electricity." We cannot argue with them here. What we must affirm, what the Church has always affirmed, is that the use of electricity may be "demonic," as in fact may be the use of anything and of life itself. That is, in other words, the experience of evil which we call *demonic* is not that of a mere absence of good, or, for that matter, of all sorts of existential alienations and anxieties. It is indeed the *presence* of dark and irrational *power*. Hatred is not merely absence of love. It is certainly more than that, and we recognize its presence as an almost physical burden that we feel in ourselves when we hate. In our world in which normal and civilized men "used electricity" to exterminate six million human beings, in this world in which right now some ten million people are in concentration camps because they failed to understand the "only way to universal happiness," in this world the "demonic" reality is not a myth. And whatever the value or the consistency of its presentation in theologies and doctrines, it is this *reality* that the Church has in mind, that it indeed *faces* when at the moment of baptism, through the hands of the priest, it lays hold upon a new human being who has just entered life, and who, according to statistics, has a great many chances some day to enter a mental institution, a penitentiary, or at best, the maddening boredom of a universal suburbia. The world from which the human being has received his life, and which will determine this life, is a prison. The Church did not have to wait for Kafka or Sartre to know it. But the Church also knows that the gates of this hell have been broken and that another Power has entered the world and claimed it for its true Owner. And that claim is not on souls alone, but on the totality of life, on the whole world. Thus —at the beginning of baptism—the Church makes that claim. The priest "breathes thrice in the face" of the catechumen, "and signeth his brow and his breast thrice with the sign of the cross and layeth his hand on the head saying:

In Thy Name, O Lord God of Truth, and in the name of thine only begotten Son, and of thy Holy Spirit, I lay my hand upon Thy servant, who has been found worthy to flee unto Thy Holy Name, and to take refuge under the shelter of Thy wings. . . . Remove far from him his former delusion, and fill him with the faith, hope and love which are in Thee; that he may know that Thou art the only true God. . . . Enable him to walk in all Thy commandments and to fulfill those things which are well pleasing unto Thee, for if a man do those things, *he shall find life in them*. Make him to rejoice in the works of his hands, and in all his generation that he may render praise unto Thee, may sing, worship and glorify Thy great and exalted Name.

The exorcisms mean this: to face evil, to acknowledge its reality, to know its power, and to proclaim the power of God to destroy it. The exorcisms announce the forthcoming baptism as an act of victory.

Then the Priest turneth the person who is come to Baptism to the west, unclad, unshod, and having his hands uplifted, and he says,—
"Dost thou renounce Satan, and all his Angels, and all his works, and all his services, and all his pride?"
And the catechumen makes answer, or his sponsor for him, and says "I do."

The first act of the Christian life is a renunciation, a challenge. No one can be Christ's until he has, first, faced evil, and then, become ready to fight it. How far is this spirit from the way in which we often proclaim, or to use a more modern term, "sell" Christianity today. Is it not usually presented as a comfort, help, release from tensions, a reasonable investment of time, energy and money? One has only to read—be it but once—the topics of the Sunday sermons announced in the Saturday newspapers, or the various syndicated "religious columns," to get the impression that "religion" is almost invariably presented as salvation from something—fear, frustration, anxiety—but never as the salvation of man and the world. How could we then speak of fight when the very set-up of our churches must, by definition, convey the idea of softness, comfort, peace? How can the Church use again the military language, which was its own in the first days, when it still thought of

itself as *militia Christi?* One does not see very well where
and how "fight" would fit into the weekly bulletin of a
suburban parish, among all kinds of refreshments and cook-
ies, counseling sessions, bake sales, and "young adult" get-
togethers.

And yet it is, indeed, the necessary condition of the next
and decisive step.

"Dost thou unite thyself unto Christ?" says the priest,
when he has turned—has *converted*—the catechumen to
the east.

Then comes the *confession of faith*, the confession by
the catechumen of the faith of the Church, of his acceptance of this faith and obedience to it. And again it is difficult to convince a modern Christian that to be the life of
the world, the Church must not "keep smiling" at the
world, putting the "all welcome" signs on the churches,
and adjusting its language to that of the last best seller. The
beginning of the Christian life—of the life in the Church—
is humility, obedience, and discipline. The last act of preparation for baptism, therefore, is this order:

"Bow down also before Him." And the Catechumen answers,
"I bow down before the Father, and the Son, and the Holy
Spirit."

3

Baptism proper begins with the blessing of the water. To
understand, however, the meaning of water here, one must
stop thinking of it as an isolated "matter" of the sacrament.

Or rather, one must realize that water is the "matter" of sacrament, because it stands for the whole of matter, is, in the baptism, the sign and presence of the world itself. In the biblical "mythological" world view—which incidentally, is more meaningful and philosophically consistent than the one offered by some "demythologizers"—water is the "*prima materia*," the basic element of the world. It is the natural symbol of life, for there is no life without water, but it is also the symbol of destruction and death, and, finally it is the symbol of purification, for there is no cleanness without it. In the Book of Genesis creation of life is presented as the liberation of the dry land from the water—as a victory of the Spirit of God over the waters—the chaos of nonexistence. In a way, then, creation is a transformation of water into life.

What is important for us, however, is that the baptismal water represents the matter of the cosmos, the world as life of man. And its blessing at the beginning of the baptismal rite acquires thus a truly cosmic and redemptive significance. God created the world and blessed it and gave it to man as his food and life, as the means of communion with him. The blessing of water signifies the return or redemption of matter to this initial and essential meaning. By accepting the baptism of John, Christ sanctified the water—made it the water of purification and reconciliation with God. It was then, as Christ was coming out of the water, that the Epiphany—the new and redemptive manifestation of God—took place, and the Spirit of God, who at the beginning of creation "moved upon the face of the waters," made water—that is, the world—again into what he made them at the beginning.

To bless, as we know already, is to give thanks. In and through thanksgiving, man acknowledges the true nature of things he receives from God, and thus makes them to be what they are. We bless and sanctify things when we offer them to God in an eucharistic movement of our whole being. And as we stand before the water—before the cosmos, the matter given to us by God—it is an all embracing eucharistic movement which gives the baptismal liturgy its true beginning.

Great art Thou, O Lord, and marvellous are Thy works, and there is no word which sufficeth to hymn Thy wonders. For Thou, of thine own good will, hast brought into being all things which before were not, and by Thy might Thou upholdest creation, and by Thy providence Thou orderest the world. . . .
Before Thee tremble all the Powers endowed with intelligence. The Sun singeth unto Thee. The moon glorifieth Thee. The stars meet together before Thy presence. The light obeyeth Thee. The deeps tremble before Thee. . . .
Thou didst come and didst save us!
We confess Thy grace. We proclaim Thy mercy. We conceal not Thy gracious acts.

Once more the world is proclaimed to be what Christ revealed and made it to be—the gift of God to man, the means of man's communion with God. This water is manifested to us as "the grace of redemption," the remission of sins, the remedy of infirmities. "For we have called upon Thy Name, O Lord, and it is wonderful, and glorious, terrible to adversaries."

It is in this water that we now baptize—i.e. immerse—
man, and this baptism is for him baptism *"into Christ"*
(Rom 6:3). For the faith in Christ that led this man to
baptism is precisely the certitude that Christ is the only
true "content"—meaning, being and end—of all that exists,
the fullness of him who fills all things. In faith the whole
world becomes the sacrament of his presence, the means of
life in him. And water, the image and presence of the world,
is truly the image and presence of Christ.

But "know you not that so many of us as were baptized
into Jesus Christ, were baptized into his death?" (Rom
6:3). Baptism— the gift of the "newness of life"—is announced as "the likeness of death." Why? Because the new
life which Christ gives to those who believe in him shone
forth from the grave. Because this world rejected Christ,
refused to see in him its own life and fulfillment. And since
it has no other life but Christ, by rejecting and killing
Christ, the world condemned itself to death. Its only ultimate reality is death, and none of the secular eschatologies
in which men still put their hope can have any force against
the simple statement of Tolstoy: "And after a stupid life
there shall come a stupid death." But the Christian is precisely the one who knows that the true reality of the world
—of *this* world, of *this* life of ours—not of some mysterious
"other" world—is in Christ; the Christian knows, rather,
that Christ *is* this reality. In its self-sufficiency the world
and all that exists in it has no meaning. And as long as we
live after the fashion of this world, as long, in other words,
as we make our life an end in itself, no meaning and no

goal stand, for they are dissolved in death. It is only when we give up freely, totally, unconditionally, the self-sufficiency of our life, when we put all its meaning in Christ, that the "newness of life"—which means a new possession of the world—is given to us. The world then truly becomes the sacrament of Christ's presence, the growth of the Kingdom and of life eternal. For Christ, "being raised from the dead, dies no more; death has no more dominion over him." Baptism is thus the death of our selfishness and self-sufficiency, and it is the "likeness of Christ's death" because *Christ's death* is this unconditional self-surrender. And as Christ's death "trampled down death" because in it the ultimate meaning and strength of life were revealed, so also does our dying with him unite us with the new "life in God."

And the meaning of this "newness of life" is manifested when the newly baptized person is clothed, immediately after baptism, in a *white garment*. It is the garment of a king. Man is again king of creation. The world is again his life, and not his death, for he knows what to do with it. He is restored to the joy and power of true human nature.

4

In the Orthodox Church, what we call today the second sacrament of initiation—that of chrismation (or confirmation)—has always been an integral part of the baptismal liturgy. For it is not so much another sacrament as the very fulfillment of baptism, its "confirmation" by the Holy

Spirit. It can be distinguished from baptism only insofar as life can be distinguished from birth. The Holy Spirit confirms the whole life of the Church because he is that life, the manifestation of the Church as the "world to come," as the joy and peace of the Kingdom. As institution, teaching, ritual, the Church is indeed not only in this world, but also of this world, a "part" of it. It is the Holy Spirit, whose coming is the inauguration, the manifestation of the ultimate, of the "last things"; who transforms the Church into the "sacrament" of the Kingdom, makes her life the presence, in this world, of the world to come.

Confirmation is thus the personal Pentecost of man, his entrance into the new life in the Holy Spirit, which is the true life of the Church. It is his ordination as truly and fully man, for to be fully man is precisely to belong to the Kingdom of God. And again, it is not his "soul" alone, his "spiritual" or "religious" life that are thus confirmed, but the totality of his human being. His whole body is anointed, sealed, sanctified, dedicated to the new life: "The seal of the gift of the Holy Spirit," says the Priest as he anoints the newly baptized, "on the brow, and on the eyes, and the nostrils, and the lips, and on both ears, and the breast and on the hands, and the feet." The whole man is now made the temple of God, and his whole life is from now on a liturgy. It is here, at this moment, that the pseudo-Christian opposition between the "spiritual" and "material," the "sacred" and the "profane," the "religious" and the "secular" is denounced, abolished, revealed as a monstrous lie about God and man and the world. The only true temple of God is man and through him the world. Each ounce of matter belongs to God and is to find in God its fulfillment. Each instant of time is God's time and is to fulfill itself as God's eternity. Nothing is "neutral." For the Holy Spirit, as a ray of light, as a smile of joy, has "touched" all things, all time—revealed all of them as precious stones of a precious temple.

To be truly man means to be fully *oneself*. The confirmation is the confirmation of man in his own, unique "personality." It is, to use again the same image, my ordination to be *myself*, to become what God wants me to be, what he has loved in me from all eternity. It is the gift of vocation. If the Church is truly the "newness of life"—the world and nature as restored in Christ—it is not, or rather, ought not be, a purely religious institution, in which to be "pious," to be a member in "good standing," means leaving one's own personality at the entrance—in the "check room"—and replacing it with a worn-out, impersonal, neutral "good Christian" type personality. Piety in fact may be a very dangerous thing, a real opposition to the Holy Spirit who is the Giver of *Life*—of joy, movement and creativity—and not of the "good conscience" which looks at everything with suspicion, fear and moral indignation.

Confirmation is the opening of man to the wholeness of divine creation, to the true *catholicity* of life. This is the "wind," the *ruah* of God entering our life, embracing it with fire and love, making us available for divine action, filling everything with joy and hope. . . .

5

We have already mentioned that in the past baptism took place on Easter—as part of the great paschal celebration. Its natural fulfillment was thus, of course, the entrance of the newly baptized into the Eucharist of the Church, the sacrament of our participation in the *Pascha* of the Kingdom. For baptism opens the doors of the Kingdom and the Holy Spirit leads us into its joy and peace, and this means into the eucharistic fulfillment. Even today, baptism and confirmation are immediately followed by a procession —which now has the form of a circular procession around the baptismal font. Originally, however, it was the procession to the doors of the Church, the procession of the entrance. It is significant that the Introit hymn of the paschal liturgy is the same which we sing as we lead the "neophyte" in the baptismal procession: "As many as have been baptized into Christ, have put on Christ, Allelulia." It is baptism, it is the baptismal Pentecost that originates the Church as procession, as entrance, as ascension into the eternal *Pascha* of the Lord.

And then, for *eight* days—the image of the fullness of time—the newly baptized were in the church, and each of those days was celebrated as Easter. On the eighth day took place the rite of the washing off of the holy chrism, the cutting of hair, and the return into the world. From the fullness of time and joy—into the time of the world as witnesses and bearers of that joy—such is the meaning of these rites, identical to the meaning of the eucharistic dismissal "let us go forth in peace. . . ." The visible signs of the sacrament are washed off—the "symbol" is to become reality, the life itself is now to be the sacramental sign, the fulfillment of the gift. And the cutting of hair—the last rite of the baptismal liturgy—is the sign that the life which now begins is a life of offering and sacrifice, the life constantly transformed into the liturgy—the work of Christ.

6

It is only in the light of baptism that we can understand the sacramental character attached by the Orthodox Church to "penance." In its juridical deviation, sacramental theology explained this sacrament in terms of sheer "juridical" power to absolve sins, a power "delegated" by Christ to the priest. But this explanation has nothing to do with the original meaning of penance in the Church, and with its sacramental nature. The sacrament of forgiveness is baptism, not because it operates a juridical removal of guilt, but because it is baptism into Jesus Christ, who is the Forgiveness. The sin of all sins—the truly "original sin"—is not a transgression of rules, but, first of all, the deviation of man's love and his alienation from God. That man preferred something—the world, himself—to God, this is the only real sin, and in it all sins became natural, inevitable. For it destroys the true life of man. It deviates life's course from its only meaning and direction. And in Christ this sin is forgiven, not in the sense that God now has "forgotten" it and pays no attention to it, but because in Christ man has *returned* to God, and has returned to God because he has loved him and found in him the only true object of love and life. And God has accepted man and—in Christ—reconciled him with himself. Repentance is thus the return of our love, of our life, to God, and this return is possible in Christ because he reveals to us the true Life and makes us aware of our exile and condemnation. To believe in Christ is to *repent*—to change radically the very "mind" of our life, to see it as sin and death. And to believe in him is to *accept* the joyful revelation that in him forgiveness and reconciliation have been given. In baptism both repentance and forgiveness find their fulfillment. In baptism man *wants* to die as a sinful man and he is given that death, and in baptism man *wants* the newness of life as forgiveness, and he is given it.

And yet, sin is still in us and we constantly fall away from the new life we have received. The fight of the new Adam against the old Adam is a long and painful one, and what a naive oversimplification to think as some do, that the "salvation" they experience in revivals and "decisions for Christ" and which result in moral righteousness, soberness and warm philanthropy, is the whole of salvation, is what God meant when he gave his Son for the life of the world. The one true sadness is "that of not being a saint," and how often the "moral" Christians are those precisely who never feel, never experience this sadness, because their own "experience of salvation," the feeling of "being saved" fills them with self-satisfaction; and whoever has been "satisfied" has received already his reward and cannot thirst and hunger for that total transformation and transfiguration of life which alone makes "saints."

Baptism is forgiveness of sins, not their removal. It introduces the sword of Christ into our life and makes it the real conflict, the inescapable pain and suffering of growth. It is indeed after baptism and because of it, that the reality of sin can be recognized in all its sadness, and true repentance becomes possible. Therefore, the whole of the Church is at the same time the gift of forgiveness, the joy of the "world to come," and also and inescapably a constant repentance. The *feast* is impossible without the *fast*, and the fast is precisely repentance and return, the saving experience of sadness and exile. The Church is the gift of the Kingdom—yet it is this very gift that makes obvious our absence from the Kingdom, our alienation from God. It is repentance that takes us again and again into the joy of the paschal banquet, but it is that joy which reveals to us our sinfulness and puts us under judgment.

The *sacrament* of *penance* is not, therefore, a sacred and juridical "power" given by God to men. It is the power of baptism as it lives in the Church. From baptism it receives its sacramental character. In Christ all sins are forgiven once and for all, for he is himself the forgiveness of sins, and there is no need for any "new" absolution. But there is indeed the need for us who constantly *leave* Christ and *excommunicate* ourselves from his life, to return to him, to receive again and again the gift which in him has been given once and for all. And the absolution is the sign that this return has taken place and has been fulfilled. And as each Eucharist is not a "repetition"—but our ascension, our acceptance into the same and eternal banquet, so also the sacrament of penance is not a repetition of baptism, but our return to the "newness of life" which God gave to us once and for all.

5 THE MYSTERY OF LOVE

"This is a great mystery: but I speak concerning Christ and the Church" (Eph 5:32)

In the Eastern Church matrimony is a sacrament. It may be asked why, of the many "states" of human life, in the great variety of man's vocations, only this "state" has been singled out and understood as a sacrament? Indeed, if it is simply a divine *sanction* of marriage, the bestowing of spiritual help to the married couple, a blessing for the procreation of children—all this does not make it radically different from any other act for which we need help and guidance, sanction and blessing. For a "sacrament," as we have seen, implies necessarily the idea of transformation, refers to the ultimate event of Christ's death and resurrection, is always a sacrament of the Kingdom. In a way, of course, the whole life of the church can be termed sacramental, for it is always the manifestation in time of the "new time." Yet in a more precise way the Church calls sacraments those decisive acts of its life in which this transforming grace is confirmed *as being given,* in which the Church through a liturgical act identifies itself with and becomes the very form of that Gift. . . . But how is marriage related to the Kingdom which is to come? How is it related to the cross, the death and resurrection of Christ? What, in other words, makes it a sacrament?

Even to raise these questions seems impossible within the whole "modern" approach to marriage, and this includes, often enough, the "Christian" approach too. In the numberless "manuals of marital happiness," in the alarming trend to make the minister a specialist in clinical sexology, in all cozy definitions of a Christian family which approve a moderate use of sex (which can be an "enriching experience") and emphasize responsibility, savings and Sunday School—in all this there is, indeed, no room for sacrament. We do not even remember today that marriage is, as everything else in "this world," a fallen and distorted marriage, and that it needs, not to be blessed and "solemnized"—after a rehearsal and with the help of the photographer—but *restored*. This restoration, furthermore, is *in Christ*—and this means in his life, death, resurrection and ascension to heaven, in the pentecostal inauguration of the "new eon," in the Church as the sacrament of all this. Needless to say, this restoration infinitely transcends the idea of the "Christian family," and gives marriage cosmic and universal dimensions.

Here is the whole point. As long as we visualize marriage as the concern of those alone who are being married, as something that happens to them and not to the whole Church, and, therefore, to the world itself, we shall never understand the truly sacramental meaning of marriage— the great mystery to which St. Paul refers when he says: "But I speak concerning Christ and the Church." We must understand that the real theme, "content" and object of this sacrament is not "family," but love. Family as such, family in itself, can be a demonic distortion of love—and there are many harsh words about it in the Gospel: "A man's foes shall be those of his own household" (Mt 10:36). In this sense the sacrament of matrimony is wider than family. It is the sacrament of divine love, as the all-embracing mystery of being itself, and it is for this reason that it concerns the whole Church, and—through the Church—the whole world.

2

But perhaps the Orthodox vision of this sacrament will be better understood if we begin not with matrimony as such, and not with an abstract "theology of love," but with the one who has always stood at the very heart of the Church's life as the purest expression of human love and response to God—Mary, the Mother of Jesus. It is significant that whereas in the West Mary is primarily the Virgin, a being almost totally different from us in her absolute and celestial purity and freedom from all carnal pollution, in the East she is always referred to and glorified as Theotokos, the Mother of God; and virtually all icons depict her with the Child in her arms. There exist, in other words, two emphases in mariology which, although they do not necessarily exclude on another, lead to two different visions of Mary's place in the Church. And the difference between them must be kept in mind if we want to understand the experience of the veneration of Mary which has always been that of the Orthodox Church. We hope to show that this is not so much a specific "cult of Mary," as a light, a joy, proper to the whole life of the Church. In her, says an Orthodox hymn, "all creation rejoices."

But what is this joy about? Why, in her own words, shall "all generations call me blessed"? Because in her love and obedience, in her faith and humility, she accepted to be what from all eternity all creation was meant and created to be: the temple of the Holy Spirit, the *humanity* of God. She accepted to give her body and blood—that is, her whole life—to be the body and blood of the Son of God, to be *mother* in the fullest and deepest sense of this word: giving her life to the Other and having, fulfilling her life in him. She accepted the only true nature of each creature and all creation: to place the meaning and, therefore, the fulfillment of her life in God.

And in accepting this nature she fulfilled the *woman-hood* of creation. This word will seem strange to many. In our time the Church, following the modern trend toward the "equality of the sexes," uses only one-half of the Christian revelation about man and woman, the one which affirms that in Christ there is neither "male nor female" (Gal 3:28). The other half is ascribed again to an anti-quated worldview. In fact, however, all these attempts to find the "place of woman" in society (or in the Church) instead of exalting her, belittle woman, for they imply too often a denial of her specific vocation as woman.

And yet is it not significant that the relation between

God and the world, between God and Israel, his chosen people, and finally between God and the cosmos restored in the Church, is expressed in the Bible in terms of marital union and love? This is a double analogy. On the one hand, we understand God's love for the world and Christ's love for the Church because we have the experience of marital love, but on the other hand, marital love has its roots, its depth and real fulfillment in the great mystery of Christ and his Church: "But I speak concerning Christ and the Church." The Church is the Bride of Christ (". . . for I have espoused you to one husband, that I may present you as a chaste virgin to Christ" Cor 11:2). This means that the world—which finds its restoration and fulfillment in the Church—is the bride of God and that in sin this fundamental relationship has been broken, distorted. And it is in Mary—the Woman, the Virgin, the Mother—in her response to God, that the Church has its living and personal beginning.

This response is total obedience in love; not obedience and love, but the wholeness of the one as the totality of the other. Obedience, taken in itself, is not a "virtue"; it is blind submission and there is no light in blindness. Eichmann claimed obedience as his justification. Only love for God, the absolute object of all love, frees obedience from blindness and makes it the joyful acceptance of that alone which is worthy of being accepted. But love without obedience to God is "the lust of the flesh, and the lust of the eyes, and the pride of life" (1 Jn 2:16), is the love claimed by Don Juan and which ultimately destroys him. Only obedience to God, the only Lord of Creation, gives love its true direction, makes it fully love.

True obedience is thus true love for God, the true response of Creation to its Creator. Humanity is fully humanity when it is this response to God, becomes the movement of total self-giving and obedience to him. But in the "natural" world the bearer of this obedient love, of the love as response, is the woman. The man proposes, the woman accepts. This acceptance is not passivity, blind submission, because it is love, and love is always active. It gives life to the proposal of man, fulfills it as life, yet it becomes fully love and fully life only when it is fully *acceptance* and *response*. This is why the whole creation, the whole Church—and not only women—find the expression of their response and obedience to God in Mary the Woman, and rejoice in her. She stands for all of us, because only when we accept, respond in love and obedience—only when we accept the essential womanhood of creation—do we become ourselves, true men and women; only then can we indeed *transcend* our limitations as "males" and "females." For man can be truly man—that is, the king of creation, the priest and minister of God's creativity and initiative—only when he does not posit himself as the "owner" of creation and accepts to submit himself—in obedience and love—to its nature as the bride of God, as *response* and *acceptance*. And woman ceases to be just a "female" when, totally and unconditionally accepting the life of the Other as *her own life*, giving herself totally to the Other, she becomes the very expression, the very fruit, the very joy, the very beauty, the very gift of our response to God, the one, whom, in the words of the Song, the king will bring into his chambers, saying: "Thou art all fair, my love, there is no spot in thee" (Ct 4:7).

Tradition calls Mary *the new Eve*. She did what the first Eve failed to do. Eve failed to be a woman. She took the initiative. She "proposed," and she became "female"— the instrument of procreation, "ruled over" by man. She made herself, and also the man whose "eve" she is, the slaves of her "femininity" and the whole of life a dark war of sexes, in which "possession" is in fact the violent and desperate desire to *kill* the shameful lust that never dies. But Mary "took no initiative." In love and obedience she expected the initiative of the Other. And when it came, she accepted it, not blindly—for she asked "how shall this be?"—but with the whole lucidity, simplicity and joy of love. The light of an eternal spring comes to us, when on the day of annunciation we hear the decisive: "Behold the handmaid of the Lord, be it unto me according to thy word" (Lk 5:38). This is indeed the whole creation, the whole humanity and each one of us recognizing the words that express our ultimate nature and being, our acceptance to be the bride of God, our betrothal to the One, who from all eternity loved us.

Mary is the *Virgin*. But this virginity is not a negation, not a mere *absence*; it is the fullness and the wholeness of love itself. It is the totality of her self-giving to God and, thus, the very expression, the very quality of her love. For

love is the thirst and hunger for wholeness, totality, fulfillment—for virginity, in the ultimate meaning of this
word. It is at the end that the Church will be presented to
Christ as a "chaste virgin" (Cor 11:2). For virginity is
the goal of all genuine love—not as absence of "sex," but
as its complete fulfillment in love; of this fulfillment in
"this world" sex is the paradoxical, the tragic affirmation
and denial. The Eastern Church by celebrating the seemingly "nonscriptural" feasts of Mary's nativity and of her
presentation to the temple reveals, in fact, a real faithful-
ness to the Bible, for the meaning of these feasts lies
precisely in their recognition of Mary the Virgin as the
goal and the fulfillment of the whole history of salvation,
of that history of love and obedience, of response and
expectation. She is the true daughter of the Old Testament,
its last and most beautiful flower. The Orthodox Church
rejects the dogma of the Immaculate Conception precisely
because it makes Mary a miraculous "break" in this long
and patient growth of love and expectation, of this "hunger
for the living God," which fills the Old Testament. She
is the gift of the world to God, as is so beautifully said
in a hymn of the nativity:

> Each of thy creatures brings thanksgiving unto Thee;
> The angels offer the sun,
> The heavens its star,
> The wise men their gifts,
> The shepherds their marveling . . .
> And we—the Virgin Mother.

And yet it is God alone who fulfils and crowns this
obedience, acceptance, and love. "The Holy Ghost shall

come upon thee and the power of the Highest shall over-
shadow thee. . . . For with God nothing shall be impossible" (Lk 1:35–37). He alone reveals as Virgin the
one who brought to him the totality of human love. . . .

Mary is the *Mother.* Motherhood is the fulfillment of
womanhood because it is the fulfillment of love as obedience and response. It is by giving herself that love gives
life, becomes source of life. One does not love *in order* to
have children. Love needs no justification; it is not because
it gives life that love is good; it is because it is good that
it gives life. The joyful mystery of Mary's motherhood
is thus not opposed to the mystery of her virginity. It is
the same mystery. She is not mother "in spite" of her
virginity. She reveals the fullness of motherhood because
her virginity is the fullness of love.

She is the *Mother of Christ.* She is the fullness of love
accepting the coming of God to us—giving life to him,
who is the Life of the world. And the whole creation rejoices in her, because it recognizes in her that the end and
fulfillment of all life, of all love *is to accept Christ,* to give
him life in ourselves. And there should be no fear that
this joy about Mary takes anything from Christ, diminishes
in any way the glory due to him and him alone. For what
we find in her and what constitutes the joy of the Church
is precisely the fullness of that adoration of Christ, of acceptance and love for him. Really, here is no "cult of
Mary," yet in Mary the "cult" of the Church becomes a
movement of joy and thanksgiving of acceptance and
obedience—the wedding to the Holy Spirit which makes
it the only complete joy on earth.

3

We can return now to the sacrament of matrimony. We can now understand that its true meaning is not that it merely gives a religious "sanction" to marriage and family life, reinforces with supernatural grace the natural family virtues. Its meaning is that by taking the "natural" marriage into "the great mystery of Christ and the Church," the sacrament of matrimony gives marriage a new meaning, transforms, in fact, not only marriage as such, but all human love.

It is worth mentioning that the early Church did not apparently know of any separate marriage service. The "fulfillment" of marriage by two Christians was their partaking together of the Eucharist. As every aspect of life was gathered into the Eucharist, so matrimony received its seal by inclusion into this central act of the community. And this means that, since marriage has always had sociological and legal dimensions, these were simply accepted by the Church. Yet, like the whole "natural" life of man, marriage had to be taken into the Church, that is, judged, redeemed and transformed in the sacrament of the Kingdom. Only later did the Church receive also the "civil" authority to perform a rite of marriage, get a "license" from the state. This meant, however, together with the recognition of the Church as the "celebrant" of matrimony, a first step in a progressive "desacramentalization." An obvious sign of this was the divorce of matrimony from the Eucharist.

All this explains why even today the Orthodox rite of matrimony consists of two distinct services: the betrothal and the crowning. The betrothal is performed not inside the Church, but in the vestibule. It is the Christian form of the "natural" marriage. It is the blessing of the rings by the priest and their exchange by the bridal pair. Yet from the very beginning this natural marriage is given its true perspective and direction: "O Lord our God," says the priest, "who hast espoused the Church as a pure Virgin from among the Gentiles, bless this Betrothal, and unite and maintain these Thy servants in peace and oneness of mind."

For the Christian, natural does not mean either self-sufficient—a "nice little family"—or merely insufficient, and to be, therefore, strengthened and completed by the addition of the "supernatural." The natural man thirsts and hungers for fulfillment and redemption. This thirst and hunger is the vestibule of the Kingdom: both beginning and exile.

Then, having blessed the natural marriage, the priest takes the bridal pair in a solemn procession into the church. This is the true form of the sacrament, for it does not merely symbolize, but indeed is the entrance of marriage into the Church, which is the entrance of the world into the "world to come," the procession of the people of God —in Christ—into the Kingdom. The rite of crowning is but a later—although beautiful and beautifully meaningful—expression of the reality of this entrance.

"O Lord and God, crown them with glory and honor!" says the priest after he has put crowns on the heads of the

bridal pair. This is, first, the glory and honor of man as
king of creation: "Be fruitful and multiply and replenish
the earth, and subdue and have dominion . . ." (Gn 1:25).
Each family is indeed a kingdom, a little church and,
therefore, a sacrament of and a way to the Kingdom. Some-
where, even if it is only in a single room, every man at
some point in his life has his own small kingdom. It may
be hell, and a place of betrayal, or it may not. Behind each
window there is a little world going on. How evident this
becomes when one is riding on a train at night and passing
innumerable lighted windows: behind each one of them
the fullness of life is a "given possibility," a promise, a
a vision. This is what the marriage crowns express: that
here is the beginning of a small kingdom which can be
something like the true Kingdom. The chance will be lost,
perhaps even in one night; but at this moment it is still
an open possibility. Yet even when it has been lost, and
lost again a thousand times, still if two people stay together,
they are in a real sense king and queen to each other. And
after forty odd years, Adam can still turn and see Eve
standing beside him, in a unity with himself which in some
small way at least, proclaims the love of God's kingdom.
In movies and magazines the "icon" of marriage is always
a youthful couple. But once, in the light and warmth of
an autumn afternoon, this writer saw on the bench of a
public square, in a poor Parisian suburb, an old and poor
couple. They were sitting hand in hand, in silence, enjoy-
ing the pale light, the last warmth of the season. In silence:
all words had been said, all passion exhausted, all storms at

peace. The whole life was behind—yet all of it was now *present*, in this silence, in this light, in this warmth, in this silent unity of hands. Present—and ready for eternity, ripe for joy. This to me remained the vision of marriage, of its heavenly beauty.

Then secondly, the glory and the honor is that of the martyr's crown. For the way to the Kingdom is the *martyria* —bearing witness to Christ. And this means crucifixion and suffering. A marriage which does not constantly crucify its own selfishness and self-sufficiency, which does not "die to itself" that it may point beyond itself, is not a Christian marriage. The real sin of marriage today is not adultery or lack of "adjustment" or "mental cruelty." It is the idoliza-tion of the family itself, the refusal to understand marriage as directed toward the Kingdom of God. This is expressed in the sentiment that one would "do anything" for his family, even steal. The family has here ceased to be for the glory of God; it has ceased to be a sacramental en-trance into his presence. It is not the lack of respect for the family, it is the idolization of the family that breaks the modern family so easily, makes divorce its almost natural shadow. It is the identification of marriage with happiness and the refusal to accept the Cross in it. In a Christian marriage, in fact, three are married; and the united loyalty of the two toward the third, who is God, keeps the two in an active unity with each other as well as with God. Yet it is the presence of God which is the death of the marriage as something only natural. It is the cross of Christ that brings the self-sufficiency of nature to

its end. But "by the cross joy (and not "happiness!")
entered the whole world." Its presence is thus the real
joy of marriage. It is the joyful certitude that the marriage
vow, in the perspective of the eternal Kingdom, is not
taken "until death parts" but until death unites us completely.

Hence the third and final meaning of the crowns: they
are the crowns of the Kingdom, of that ultimate Reality
of which everything in "this world"—whose fashion passeth away—everything has now become a sacramental sign
and anticipation. "Receive their crowns in Thy Kingdom,"
says the priest, as he removes them from the heads of the
newly wed and this means: make this marriage a growth
in that perfected love of which God alone is the end and
fullness.

The common cup given to the couple after the crowning
is explained today as a symbol of "common life," and
nothing shows better the "descramentalization" of marriage, its reduction to a "natural happiness." In the past
this was communion, the partaking of the Eucharist, the
ultimate *seal* of the fulfillment of marriage in Christ. Christ
is to be the very essence of life together. He is the wine of
the new life of the children of God, and communion in it
will proclaim how, by getting older and older in this
world, we are growing younger and younger in the life
which has no evening.

As the wedding service is completed, the bride and
bridegroom join hands and follow the priest in a procession
around the table. As in baptism, this procession in a circle

signifies the eternal journey which has begun; marriage will be a procession hand in hand, a continuation of that which has started here, not always joyful, but always capable of being referred to and filled with joy.

4

Nowhere is the truly universal, truly cosmic significance of the sacrament of matrimony, as the sacrament of love, expressed better than in its liturgical similitude with the liturgy of ordination, the sacrament of priesthood. It is not a mere identity of ritual symbolism. Through it is revealed the identity of the Reality to which both sacraments refer, of which both are the manifestation.

Centuries of "clericalism" (and one should not think of clericalism as a monopoly of the "hierarchical" and "liturgical" churches) have made the priest, the minister a *being apart*, a unique and specifically "sacred" vocation in the Church. This vocation is not only different from—it is indeed opposed to, all of those that are "profane." Such was, such still is the secret spring of sacerdotal psychology and training. It is not accidental, therefore, that the words "laity," "layman" became little by little synonymous with a lack of something in a man, or his *nonbelonging*. Yet originally the words "laity," "layman" referred to the *laos*—the people of God—and were not only positive in meaning, but included the "clergy." But today one who says he is a layman in physics acknowledges his ignorance of this science, his nonbelonging to the closed circle of specialists.

For centuries the clerical state was exalted as virtually a "supernatural" one and there is a slight connotation of mystical awe when a man says: "People should respect the clergy." And if some day a science which has been long overdue—pastoral pathology—is taught in the seminaries, its first discovery might be that some "clerical vocations" are in fact rooted in a morbid desire for that "supernatural respect," especially when the chances of a "natural" one are slim. Our secular world "respects" clergy as it respects cemeteries: both are needed, both are sacred, both are out of life.

But what both clericalism and secularism—the former being, in fact, the natural father of the latter—have made us forget is that to be *priest* is from a profound point of view, the most natural thing in the world. Man was created priest of the world, the one who offers the world to God in a sacrifice of love and praise and who, through this eternal eucharist, bestows the divine love upon the world. Priesthood, in this sense, is the very essence of manhood, man's creative relation to the "womanhood" of the created world. And Christ is the one true Priest because he is the one true and perfect man. He is the new Adam, the restoration of that which Adam failed to be. Adam failed to be the priest of the world and because of this failure, the world ceased to be the sacrament of the divine love and presence, and became "nature." And in this "natural" world religion became an organized transaction with the supernatural, and the priest was set apart as the "transactor," as the mediator between the natural and the supernatural. And after all, it does not matter too much whether this mediation was understood in terms of magic—as supernatural powers—or in terms of law—as supernatural rights.

But Christ revealed the essence of priesthood to be love and, therefore, priesthood to be the essence of life. He died, the last victim of the priestly religion, and in his death the priestly *religion* died and the priestly *life* was inaugurated. He was killed by the priests, by the "clergy," but his sacrifice abolished them as it abolished "religion." And it abolished religion because it destroyed that wall of separation between the "natural" and the "supernatural," the "profane" and the "sacred," the "this-worldly" and the "other-worldly"—which was the only justification and *raison d'etre* of religion. He revealed that all things, all nature have their end, their fulfillment in the Kingdom, that all things are to be made new by love.

And if there are priests in the Church, if there is the priestly vocation in it, it is precisely in order to reveal to each vocation its priestly essence, to make the whole life of all men the liturgy of the Kingdom, to reveal the Church as the royal priesthood of the redeemed world. It is, in other terms, not a vocation "apart," but the expression of love for man's vocation as son of God and for the world as the sacrament of the Kingdom. And there must be priests because we live in *this world*, and nothing in it is the Kingdom and, as "this world," will never become the Kingdom. The Church is in the world but not of the world, because only by *not* being of the world can it reveal and manifest the "world to come," the beyond, which alone reveals all things as *old*—yet new and eternal in the love of God. Therefore, no vocation in *this world* can fulfill itself as priesthood. And thus there must be the one whose specific vocation *is to have no vocation*, to be *all things to all men*, and to reveal thus that the end and the meaning of all things are in Christ.

No one can take it upon himself to become a priest, to decide it on the basis of his own qualifications, preparation and predispositions. The vocation always comes from above —from God's ordination and order. The priesthood reveals the humility, not the pride, of the Church, for it reveals the complete dependence of the Church on Christ's love, that is, on his unique and perfect priesthood. It is not "priesthood" that the priest receives in his ordination, but the gift of Christ's love, that love which made Christ the only Priest and which fills with this unique priesthood the ministry of those whom he sends to his people.

This is why the sacrament of ordination is, in a sense, identical with the sacrament of matrimony. Both are the manifestation of love. The priest is indeed married to the Church. But just as the human marriage is taken into the mystery of Christ and the Church, and becomes the sacrament of the Kingdom, it is this marriage of the priest with the Church that makes him really *priest*, the true minister of that Love which alone transforms the world and reveals the Church as the immaculate bride of Christ.

The final point is this: some of us are married and some are not. Some of us are called to be priests and ministers and some are not. But the sacraments of matrimony and priesthood concern all of us, because they concern our life as *vocation*. The meaning, the essence and the end of all vocation is *the mystery of Christ and the Church*. It is through the Church that each one of us finds that the vocation of all vocations is to follow Christ in the fullness of his priesthood: in his love for man and the world, his love for their ultimate fulfillment in the abundant life of the Kingdom.

6 Trampling Down Death by Death

We live today in a death-denying culture. This is clearly seen in the unobtrusive appearance of the ordinary funeral home, in its attempt to look like all other houses. Inside, the "funeral director" tries to take care of things in such a way that one will not notice that one is sad; and a parlor ritual is designed to transform a funeral into a semi-pleasant experience. There is a strange conspiracy of silence concerning the blunt fact of death, and the corpse itself is "beautified" so as to disguise its deadness. But there existed in the past and there still exist—even within our life-affirming modern world—"death-centered" cultures, in which death is the one great all embracing preoccupation, and life itself is conceived as being mainly preparation for death. If to some the funeral home itself seems to divert thoughts from death, to some others even the "utilities" such as a bed or a table become symbols, reminders of death. A bed is seen as the image of the grave, the casket is put on the table.

Where is Christianity in all this? There can be no doubt, on the one hand, that the "problem of death" is central and essential in its message, which announces Christ's victory over death, that Christianity has its source in that victory. Yet, on the other hand, one has the strange feeling that although this message has certainly been heard, it has had no real impact on the basic human attitudes toward death. It is rather Christianity that has "adjusted" itself to these attitudes, accepted them as its own. It is not difficult to dedicate to God—in a nice Christian sermon—new skyscrapers and world's fairs, to join—if not to lead—the great progressive and life-affirming forces of our "atomic age," to make Christianity appear as the very source of all this hectic and life-centered activity. And it is equally easy, when preaching at a funeral or a retreat, to present life as a valley of suffering and vanity, and to present death— as a liberation.

A Christian minister, representative in this of the whole Church, must today use *both languages*, espouse both attitudes. But if he is sincere he must inescapably feel that "something is missing" in both, and that this is in fact *the* Christian element itself. For it falsifies the Christian message to present and to preach Christianity as essentially life-affirming—without referring this affirmation to the death of Christ and, therefore to the very fact of death; to pass over in silence the fact that, for Christianity death is not only the end, but indeed, the very reality of *this world*. But to "comfort" people and reconcile them with death by making this world a meaningless scene of an individual preparation for death is also to falsify it. For Christianity proclaims that Christ died for the life of the world, and not for an "eternal rest" from it. This "falsification" makes the very success of Christianity (according to official data

church building and per capita contributions to churches
have reached an all time high!) into a profound tragedy.
The worldly man wants the minister to be an optimistic
fellow, sanctioning faith in an optimistic and progressive
world. And the religious man sees him as an utterly serious,
sadly solemn and dignified denouncer of the world's vanity
and futility. The world does not want religion and religion
does not want Christianity. The one rejects death, the
other, life. Hence the immense frustration either with
the secularistic tendencies of the life-affirming world or
with the morbid religiosity of those who oppose it.

This frustration will last as long as Christians continue
to understand Christianity as a religion whose purpose is
to *help*, as long as they continue to keep the "utilitarian"
self-consciousness typical of the "old" religion. For this
was, indeed, one of the main functions of religions: to
help, and especially to help people to die. For this reason
religion has always been an attempt to *explain* death and,
by explaining it, to reconcile man with it. What pains
Plato took in his *Phaedo* to make death desirable and even
good, and how often he has since been echoed in the history of human belief when confronted with the prospect
of release from this world of change and suffering! Men
have consoled themselves with the rationalization that God
made death and that it is therefore right, or with the fact
that death belongs to the pattern of life; they have found
various meanings in death, or assured themselves that
death is preferable to decrepit old age; they have formu-
lated doctrines of the immortality of the soul—that if a

man dies, at least a part of him survives. All this has been one long attempt to take the awful uniqueness out of the experience of death.

Christianity, because it is a *religion*, had to accept this fundamental function of religion: to "justify" death and thus to *help*. In doing so, moreover, it more or less assimulated the old and classical explanations of death, common to virtually all religions. For neither the doctrine of the immortality of the soul, based on the opposition between the spiritual and the material, nor that of death as liberation, nor of death as punishment, are, in fact Christian doctrines. And their integration into the Christian world-view vitiated rather than clarified Christian theology and piety. They "worked" as long as Christianity lived in a religious (i.e. death-centered) world. But they cease to work as soon as the world outgrows this old death-centered religion and becomes "secular." Yet the world has become secular not because it has become "irreligious," "materialistic," "superficial," not because it has "lost religion"— as so many Christians still think—but because old explanations do not really explain. Christians often do not realize that they themselves, or rather Christianity, has been a major factor in this liberation from the old religion. Christianity with its message offering fullness of life, has contributed more than anything else to the liberation of man from the fears and the pessimism of religion. Secularism, in this sense, is a phenomenon within the Christian world, a phenomenon impossible without Christianity. Secularism rejects Christianity insofar as Christianity has identified itself with the "old religion" and is forcing upon the world those "explanations" and "doctrines" of death and life which Christianity has itself destroyed.

It would be a great mistake, however, to think of secularism as simply an "absence of religion." It is, in fact, itself a religion, and as such, an explanation of death and a reconciliation with it. It is the religion of those who are tired of having the world explained in terms of an "other world" of which no one knows anything, and life explained in terms of a "survival" about which no one has the slightest idea; tired of having, in other words, life given "value" in terms of death. Secularism is an "explanation" of death in terms of life. The only world we know is this world, the only life given to us is this life—and it is up to us men to make it as meaningful, as rich, as happy as possible. Life ends with death. This is unpleasant, but since it is natural, since death is an universal phenomenon, the best thing man can do about it, is simply to accept it as something natural. As long as he lives, however, he need not think about it, but live, in other words, as if death did not exist. The best way to forget about death is to be busy, to be useful, to be dedicated to great and noble things, to build an always better world. If God exists (and a great many secularists firmly believe in God and the usefulness of religion for their corporate and individual enterprises) and if he, in his love and mercy (for we all have our shortcomings) wants to reward us for our busy, useful and righteous life with eternal vacations, traditionally called "immortality," it is strictly his gracious business. But immortality is an appendix (however eternal) to this life in which all real interests, all true values are to be found. The American "funeral home" is indeed the very symbol of secularist religion, for it expresses both the quiet acceptance of death as something natural (a house among other houses with nothing typical about it) and the denial of death's presence in life.

Secularism is a religion because it has a faith, it has its own eschatology and its own ethics. And it "works" and it "helps." Quite frankly, if "help" were the criterion, one would have to admit that life-centered secularism *helps* actually more than religion. To compete with it, religion has to present itself as "adjustment to life," "counselling," "enrichment," to be publicized in subways and buses as a valuable addition to "your friendly bank" and all other "friendly dealers": try it, it *helps!* And the religious success of secularism is so great that it leads some Christian theologians to "give up" the very category of "transcendence," or in much simpler words, the very idea of "God." This is the price we must pay if we want to be "understood" and "accepted" by modern man—proclaim the Gnostics of the twentieth century.

But it is here that we reach the heart of the matter. For Christianity *help* is not the criterion. Truth is the criterion. The purpose of Christianity is not to help people by reconciling them with death, but to reveal the Truth about life and death in order that people may be saved by this Truth. Salvation, however, is not only not identical with help, but is, in fact, opposed to it. Christianity quarrels with religion and secularism not because they offer "insufficient help," but because precisely they "suffice," because they "satisfy" the needs of men. If the purpose of Christianity were to take away from man the fear of death, to reconcile him with death, there would be no need for Christianity, for each religion has done this, indeed, better than Christianity. And secularism is about to produce a man who will gladly and corporately die—and not just live—for the triumph of the Cause, whatever it may be.

Christianity is not reconciliation with death. It is the revelation of death, and it reveals death because it is the revelation of Life. Christ is this Life. And only if Christ is Life is death what Christianity proclaims it to be, namely the enemy to be destroyed, and not a "mystery" to be explained. Religion and secularism by explaining death give it a "status," a rationale, make it "normal." Only Christianity proclaims it to be *abnormal* and, therefore, truly horrible. At the grave of Lazarus Christ wept. And when his own hour to die approached, "he began to be sore amazed and very heavy." In the light of Christ, *this* world, this *life* are lost and are beyond mere "help," not because there is fear of death in them, but because they have accepted and normalized death. To accept God's world as a cosmic cemetery which is to be abolished and replaced by an "other world" which looks like a cemetery ("eternal rest") and to call this religion, to live in a cosmic cemetery and to "dispose" every day of thousands of corpses and to get excited about a "just society" and to be happy!—this is the fall of man. It is not the immortality or the crimes of man that reveal him as a fallen being; it is his "positive ideal"—

religious or secular—and his satisfaction with this ideal. This fall, however, can be truly revealed only in Christ, because only in Christ is the *fullness of life* revealed to us, and death, therefore, becomes "awful," the very fall from life, the enemy. It is *this world* (and not any "other world"), it is *this* life (and not some "other life") that were given to man to be a sacrament of the divine presence, given as communion with God, and it is only through this world, this life, by "transforming" them into communion with God that man *was*. The horror of death is, therefore, not in its being the "end" and not in physical destruction. By being separation from the world and life, it is separation *from God*. The dead cannot glorify God. It is, in other words, when Christ reveals Life to us that we can hear the Christian message about death as the enemy of God. It is when life weeps at the grave of the friend, when it contemplates the horror of death, that the victory over death begins.

2

Before death, however, there is *dying*; the growth of death in us in physical decay and illness. Here again the Christian approach cannot be simply identified either with that of the modern world, or with the one that characterizes "religion." For the modern secular world, health is the only *normal* state of man; disease, therefore is to be fought and the modern world fights it very well, indeed. Hospitals and medicine, in general, are one of its best achievements.

Health has a limit and it is death. There comes a time when the "resources of science" are exhausted—and this the modern world accepts as simply, as lucidly as it accepts death itself. There comes a moment when the patient is to be surrendered to death, to be removed from the ward, and this is done quietly, properly, hygienically as part of the general routine. As long as a man is alive everything is to be done to keep him alive, and even if his case is hopeless, it must not be revealed to him. Death must never be part of life. And although everyone knows that people die in hospitals, their general tone and ethos are those of cheerful optimism. The object of modern medicine's efficient care is life, and not mortal life.

The religious outlook considers disease rather than health to be the "normal" state of man. In this world of mortal and changing matter suffering, sickness and sorrow are the normal conditions of life. Hospitals and medical care must be supplied, but as a religious duty and not because of any real interest in health as such. Health and healing are always thought of as the mercy of God, from the religious point of view, and real healing is "miraculous." And this miracle is performed by God, again not because health is good, but because it "proves" the power of God and brings men back to God.

In their ultimate implications these two approaches are incompatible, and nothing reveals better the confusion of Christians on this issue than the fact that today Christians accept both of them as equally valid and true. The problem of a secular hospital is solved by establishing a Christian chaplaincy in it, and the problem of a Christian hospital by

making it as modern and scientific—that is, as "secular"—
as possible. In fact, however, there is a progressive surrender
of the religious approach to the secular, for reasons which we
have already analyzed above. The modern minister tends to
become not only an "assistant" to the medical doctor, but
a "therapist" in his own right. All kinds of techniques of
pastoral therapy, hospital visiting, care of the "sick"—which
fill the catalogues of theological seminaries—are a good in-
dication of this. But is this the Christian approach—and if
it is not, are we simply to return to the old—the "religious"
one?

The answer is no, it is not; but we are not simply to
"return." We must discover the unchanging, yet always
contemporary, sacramental vision of man's life and therefore of his suffering and disease, the vision that has been
the Church's, even if we Christians have forgotten or misunderstood it.

The Church considers healing as a sacrament. But such
was its misunderstanding during the long centuries of the
total identification of the Church with "religion" (misunderstanding from which suffered all sacraments and the
whole doctrine of sacraments) that the sacrament of oil
became in fact the sacrament of death, one of the "last
rites" opening to man a more or less safe passage into
eternity. There is a danger that today, with the growing
interest in healing among Christians, it will be understood
as a sacrament of health, a useful "complement" to secular
medicine. And both views are wrong, because both miss
precisely the sacramental nature of this act.

A sacrament—as we already know—is always a passage,

a *transformation*. Yet it is not a "passage" into "supernature," but into the Kingdom of God, the world to come, into the very reality of this world and its life as redeemed and restored by Christ. It is the transformation not of "nature" into "supernature," but of the *old* into the *new*. A sacrament, thus, is not a "miracle" by which God breaks, so to speak, the "laws of nature," but the manifestation of the ultimate Truth about the world and life, man and nature, the Truth which is Christ.

And healing is a sacrament because its purpose or end is not *health* as such, the restoration of physical health, but the *entrance* of man into the life of the Kingdom, into the "joy and peace" of the Holy Spirit. In Christ everything in this world, and this means health and disease, joy and suffering, has become an ascension to, and entrance into this new life, its expectation and anticipation.

In this world suffering and disease are indeed "normal," but their very "normalcy" is abnormal. They reveal the ultimate and permanent defeat of man and of life, defeat which no partial victories of medicine, however wonderful and truly miraculous, can ultimately overcome. But in Christ suffering is not "removed"; it is transformed into victory. The defeat *itself* becomes victory, a way, an entrance into the Kingdom, and this is the only true *healing*.

Here is a man suffering on his bed of pain and the Church comes to him to perform the sacrament of healing. For this man, as for every man and the whole world, suffering can be *the* defeat, the way of a complete surrender to darkness, despair and solitude. It can be *dying* in the very real sense of the word. And yet it can be also the ultimate victory of Man and of Life in him. The Church does not come to restore *health* in this man, simply to replace medicine when medicine has exhausted its own possibilities. The Church coms to take this man into the Love, the Light and the Life of Christ. It comes not merely to "comfort" him in his sufferings, not to "help" him, but to make him a *martyr*, a *witness* to Christ in his very sufferings. A martyr is one who beholds "the heavens opened, and the Son of Man standing on the right hand of God" (Acts 7:56). A martyr is one for whom God is not another—and the last—chance to stop the awful pain; God is his very life, and thus everything in his life comes to God, ascends to the fullness of Love.

In *this world* there shall be tribulation. Whether reduced to a minimum by man himself, or given some relief by the religious promise of a reward in the "other world," suffering remains here, it remains awfully "normal." And yet Christ says, "be of good cheer, I have overcome the world" (Jn 16:33). On his own suffering, not only has all suffering acquired a meaning; it has been given the power to become itself the sign, the sacrament, the proclamation, the "coming" of that victory; the defeat of man, his very *dying* has become a way of Life.

3

And the beginning of this victory is Christ's death. Such is the eternal gospel, and it remains "foolishness" not only for *this world*, but also for *religion* as long as it is religion of this world. "Lest the cross of Christ should be made of no effect" (1 Cor 1:17). The liturgy of Christian death does not begin when a man has come to the inescapable end and his corpse lies in church for the last rites while we stand around, the sad yet resigned witnesses of the dignified removal of a man from the world of the living. It begins every Sunday as the Church ascending into heaven, "puts aside all earthly care"; it begins every feast day; it begins especially in the joy of Easter. The whole life of the Church is in a way the sacrament of our death, because all of it is the proclamation of the Lord's death, the confession of his resurrection. And yet Christianity is not a death-centered religion; it is not a "mystery cult" in which an "objective" doctrine of salvation from death is offered to me in beautiful ceremonies and requires that I believe in it and thus profit of its "benefits."

To be Christian, to believe in Christ, means and has always meant this: to know in a transrational and yet absolutely certain way called faith, that Christ is the Life of all life, that he is Life itself and, therefore, my life. "In him was life; and the life was the light of men." All Christian doctrines—those of incarnation, redemption, atonement—are explanations, consequences, but not the "cause" of that faith. Only when we believe in Christ do all these affirmations become "valid" and "consistent." But faith itself is the acceptance not of this or that "proposition" about Christ, but of Christ himself as the Life and the light of life. "For the life was manifested and we have seen it, and bear witness, and show unto you that eternal life, which was with the Father, and was manifested unto us." In this sense

Christian faith is radically different from "religious belief."
Its starting point is not "belief" but love. In itself and by
itself all belief is partial, fragmentary, fragile. "For we know
in part, and we prophesy in part . . . whether there be
prophecies, they shall fail; whether there be tongues, they
shall cease; whether there be knowledge, it shall vanish
away." Only *love never faileth* (1 Cor 13). And if to love
someone means that I have my life in him, or rather that
he has become the "content" of my life, to love Christ is
to know and to possess him as the Life of my life.

Only this possession of Christ as Life, the "joy and
peace" of communion with him, the certitude of his presence, makes meaningful the proclamation of Christ's death
and the confession of his resurrection. In *this world* Christ's
resurrection can never be made an "objective fact." The
risen Lord appeared to Mary and "she saw him standing
and knew not it was Jesus." He stood on the shore of the
Sea of Tiberias "but the disciples knew not it was Jesus."
And on the way to Emmaus the eyes of the disciples "were
holden that they should not know him." The preaching of
the resurrection remains foolishness to this world and no
wonder even Christians themselves somehow "explain it
away" by virtually reducing it to the old pre-Christian doctrines of immortality and survival. And indeed, if the doctrine of resurrection is just a "doctrine," if it is to be believed in as an event of the "future," as a mystery of the
"other world," it is not substantially different from the
other doctrines concerning the "other world" and can be
easily confused with them. Whether it is the immortality

of the soul or the resurrection of the body—I know nothing of them and all discussion here is mere "speculation." Death remains the same mysterious passage into a mysterious future. The *great joy* that the disciples felt when they saw the risen Lord, this "burning of heart" that they experienced on the way to Emmaus was not because the mysteries of an "other world" were revealed to them. It was *because* they saw the Lord. And he sent them to preach and to proclaim not the resurrection of the dead—not a doctrine of death—but repentance and remission of sins, the new life, the Kingdom. They announced what they knew, that in Christ the *new life* has already begun, that he is Life Eternal, the Fulfillment, the Resurrection and the Joy of the world.

The Church is the entrance into the risen life of Christ, communion in life eternal, "joy and peace in the Holy Spirit." And it is the expectation of the "day without evening" of the Kingdom; not of any "other world," but of the fulfillment of all things and all life in Christ. In him death itself has become an act of life, for he has filled it with himself, with his love and light. In him "all things are yours; whether . . . the world, or life, or death, or things present, or things to come; all are yours; and ye are Christ's; and Christ is God's" (1 Cor 3:21–23). And if I make this *new life* mine, mine this hunger and thirst of the Kingdom, mine this expectation of Christ, mine the certitude that Christ is Life, my very death will be an act of communion with Life. For neither Life nor death can separate us from the love of Christ. I do not know when and how the fulfill-

ment will come. I do not know when all things will be consummated in Christ. I know nothing about the "whens"
and "hows." But I know that in Christ this great Passage,
the *Pascha* of the world has begun, that the light of the
"world to come" comes to us in the joy and peace of the
Holy Spirit, for *Christ is risen and Life reigneth.*

7 AND YE ARE WITNESSES
OF THESE THINGS

There is no need to repeat here what has been said so often and so well in these last years: that the Church is mission and that to be mission is its very essence, its very life. There is need, however, to remind ourselves of certain "dimensions" of Christian mission that have often been forgotten since the Church accepted its *establishment* in the world, the respectable position of a "world religion."

But, first, a few words about our present missionary situation. Whatever the achievements of the Christian mission in the past, today we must honestly face a double failure: the failure to achieve any substantial "victory" over the other great world religions and the failure to overcome in any significant way the prevailing and the growing secularism of our culture. In regard to other religions Christianity stands simply as one of them, and the time is certainly gone when Christians could consider them as "primitive" and bound to disappear when exposed to the self-evident "superiority" of Christianity. Not only have they not disappeared, but they show today a remarkable vitality and they "proselytize" even within our so-called Christian society. As to secularism, nothing shows better our inability to cope with it than the confusion and division it provokes among Christians themselves; the total and violent rejection of secularism in all varieties of Christian "fundamentalism" clashes with its almost enthusiastic acceptance by the numerous Christian interpreters of the "modern world" and "modern man." Hence the unending reassessments by Christians of their missionary task and methods, of their place and function in the world.

Here two main streams or tendencies may be discerned. There is, first, the *religious* approach of which we have already spoken in the first chapter. The object of mission is thought of as the propogation of *religion*, considered to be an essential need of man. What is significant here is that even the most traditional, confessional and "exclusive" churches accept the idea of a *modus vivendi* with other religions, of all kinds of "dialogues" and "rapprochements." There exist—such is the assumption—a basic religion, some basic "religious" and "spiritual values," and they must be defended against atheism, materialism and other forms of irreligion. Not only "liberal" and "nondenominational," but also the most conservative Christians are ready to give up the old idea of mission as the preaching of the one, true universal religion, opposed as such to all other religions, and replace it by a common front of all religions against *the* enemy: secularism. Since all religions are threatened by its victorious growth, since religion and the "spiritual values" are on the decline, religious men of all faiths must forget their quarrels and unite in defending these values.

But what are these "basic religious values"? If one analyzes them honestly, one does not find a single one that would be "basically" different from what secularism at its best also proclaims and offers to men. Ethics? Concern for truth? Human brotherhood and solidarity? Justice? Abnegation? In all honesty, there is more of passionate concern for all these "values" among "secularists" than within the organized religious bodies which so easily accommodate themselves to ethical minimalism, intellectual indifference, superstitions, dead traditionalism. What remains is the famous "anxiety" and the numberless "personal problems" in which religion claims to be supremely competent. But even here is it not highly significant—and we have spoken of this already—that when dealing with these "problems" religion has to borrow the whole arsenal and terminology of various secular "therapeutics"? Are not, for instance, the "values" stressed in both manuals of marital happiness—a religious and a secular one—in fact identical, as are also the language, the images and the proposed techniques?

It sounds like a paradox, but the basic religion that is being preached and accepted as the only means of overcoming secularism is in reality a surrender to secularism. This surrender can take place—and actually does—in all Christian confessions, although it is differently "colored" in a nondenominational suburban "community church" and in a traditional, hierarchical, confessional and liturgical parish. For the surrender consists not in giving up creeds, traditions, symbols and customs (of all this the secular man, tired of his functional office, is sometimes extremely fond), but in accepting the very function of religion in terms which are, in fact, those of secularism—as *help*, be it help in character building, peace of mind, or assurance of eternal salvation. It is in this "key" that religion is preached to, and accepted by, millions and millions of average believers today. And it is really amazing how little difference exists in the religious self-consciousness of members of confessions whose dogmas seem to stand in radical opposition to one another. For even if a man changes religion, it is usually because he finds the one he accepts as offering him "more help"—not more truth. While religious leaders are discussing ecumenicity at the top, there exists already at the grass roots a real ecumenicity in this "basic religion." It is here, in this "key" that we find the source of the apparent success of religions in some parts of the world, such as America, where the religious "boom" is due primarily to the secularization of religion. It is also the source of the decline of religion in those parts of the world where man has not time enough yet for constant analysis of his anxieties and where "secularism" still holds out the great promise of bread and freedom.

But if this is religion, its decline will continue, whether it takes the form of a direct abandonment of religion, or that of the understanding of religion as an appendix to a world which has long ago ceased to refer itself and all its activity to God. And in this general religious decline, the non-Christian "great religions" have an even greater chance of survival. For it may be asked whether certain non-Christian "spiritual traditions" are not really of "greater help" from the standpoint of what men today expect from religion. Islam and Buddhism offer excellent religious "satisfaction" and "help" not only to primitive men, but to the

most sophisticated intellectual as well. Have not Oriental
wisdom and Oriental *mysticism* always exercised an almost
irresistible attraction for religious people everywhere? It is
to be feared that certain "mystical" aspects of Eastern
Orthodoxy owe their growing popularity in the West precisely to their easy—although wrong—identification with
Oriental mysticism. The ascetical writings collected in the
Philocalia have a tremendous success in some esoteric
groups that are supremely indifferent to the life, death, and
resurrection of Jesus Christ. And the spiritual preoccupa-
tions of those esoteric groups are, in the last analysis, not
very different from those of the most emphatically Christ-
centered preachers of personal salvation and "assurance of
life eternal." In both instances what is offered is a "spiritual
dimension" of life which leaves intact and unaltered the
"material dimension"—that is, the world itself—and leaves
it intact without any bad conscience. It is a very serious
question, indeed, whether under its seemingly traditional
cover certain forms of contemporary Christian mission do
not in reality pave the way for a "world religion" that will
have very little in common with the faith that once over-
came the world.

2

The second tendency consists in the accepance of secularism. According to the ideologists of a "nonreligious" Christianity, secularism is not the enemy, not the fruit of man's
tragic loss of religion, not a sin and a tragedy, but the

world's "coming of age" which Christianity must acknowledge and accept as perfectly normal: "Honesty demands that we recognize that we must live in the world as if there were no God." This point of view has recently been developed in several remarkable books and there is no need to expound it here. The important thing for us is that mission is understood here primarily in terms of human solidarity. A Christian is a "man-for-the other." He shares completely and unconditionally in human life within a perspective conveyed to him by the story of Jesus of Nazareth. Christian mission is not to preach Christ, but to be Christians in life.

There are, no doubt, very valuable "emphases" in this trend. And first of all, secularism must indeed be acknowledged as a "Christian" phenomenon, as a result of the Christian revolution. It can be explained only within the context of the history whose starting point is the encounter between Athens and Jerusalem. It is indeed one of the grave errors of religious anti-secularism that it does not see that secularism is made up of *verités chrétiennes devenues folles*, of Christian truths that "went mad," and that in simply rejecting secularism, it in fact rejects with it certain fundamentally Christian aspirations and hopes. It is true that through "secularization," and not in direct religious encounter with Christianity, men of other "great religions" can understand certain dimensions of thought and experience without which Christianity cannot be "heard." It is true also that in its historical development, Christianity has returned to the pre-Christian and fundamentally non-Chris-

tian dichotomies of the "sacred" and "profane," spiritual
and material, etc., and has thus narrowed and vitiated its
own message.

And yet when all this is acknowledged there remains the
ultimate truth, to which the Christian partisans of secularization seem to be blind. This truth is that secularism—and
precisely because of its Christian "origin," because of the
indelible Christian seal on it—is a tragedy and a sin. It is
tragedy because having tasted a good wine, man preferred
and still prefers to return to plain water; having seen the
true light, he has chosen the light of his own logics. It is
indeed characteristic that the prophets and the preachers
of "secularized Christianity" constantly refer to "modern
man" as the one who "uses electricity" and who is shaped
by "industrialism" and the "scientific worldview." Poetry
and art, music and dancing are not included. The "modern
man" has "come of age" as a deadly serious adult, conscious
of his sufferings and alienations, but not of joy, of sex but
not of love, of science but not of "mystery." Since he knows
there is no "heaven," he cannot understand the prayer to
our Father who is in heaven, and the affirmation that
heaven and earth are full of his glory. But the tragedy is
also a sin, because secularism is a lie about the world. "To
live in the world as if there were no God!"—but honesty to
the Gospel, to the whole Christian tradition, to the experience of every saint and every word of Christian liturgy demands exactly the opposite: to live in the world seeing
everything in it as a revelation of God, a sign of his presence,
the joy of his coming, the call to communion with him,

the hope for fulfillment in him. Since the day of Pentecost there is a seal, a ray, a sign of the Holy Spirit on everything for those who believe in Christ and know that he is the life of the world—and that in him the world in its totality has become again a *liturgy*, a *communion*, an *ascension*. To *accept* secularism as the *truth* about the world is, therefore, to change the original Christian faith so deeply and so radically, that the question must be asked: do we really speak of the same Christ?

3

The only purpose of this book has been to show, or rather to "signify" that the choice between these two reductions of Christianity—to "religion" and to "secularism"—is not the only choice, that in fact it is a false dilemma. "And ye are witnesses to these things. . . ." To what things? In a language that can never be adequate, we have tried to speak about them. And it is our certitude that in the ascension of the Church in Christ, in the joy of the world to come, in the Church as the *sacrament*—the gift, the beginning, the presence, the promise, the reality, the anticipation—of the Kingdom, is the source and the beginning of all Christian mission. It is only as we return from the light and the joy of Christ's presence that we recover the world as a meaningful field of our Christian action, that we see the true reality of the world and thus discover what we must do. Christian mission is always at its beginning. It is today that I am sent back into the world *in joy and peace*, "having seen the true light," having partaken of the Holy Spirit, having been witness of divine Love.

What am I going to do? What are the Church and each Christian to do in this world? What is our *mission*?

To these questions there exist no answers in the form of practical "recipes." "It all depends" on thousands of factors —and, to be sure, all faculties of our human intelligence and wisdom, organization and planning, are to be constantly used. And yet—and this is the one "point" we wanted to make in these pages—"it all depends" primarily on our being real witnesses of the joy and peace of the Holy Spirit, of that new life of which we are made partakers in the Church. The Church is the sacrament of the Kingdom —not because it possesses divinely instituted acts called "sacraments," but because first of all, it is the possibility given to man to see in and through this world the "world to come," to see and to "live" it in Christ. It is only when, in the darkness of *this world*, we discern that Christ has *already* "filled all things with Himself," that these *things*, whatever they may be, are revealed and given to us as full of meaning and beauty. A Christian is the one who, wherever he looks, finds everywhere Christ, and rejoices in Him. And this joy *transforms* all his human plans and programs, decisions and moves, makes all his mission the sacraments of the world's return to Him, who is the life of the world.